EDDIE ROSS
MODERN *mix*

CURATING PERSONAL STYLE
WITH CHIC & ACCESSIBLE FINDS

WITH
JAITHAN KOCHAR
FOREWORD BY BUNNY WILLIAMS

GIBBS SMITH
TO ENRICH AND INSPIRE HUMANKIND

"Not all of us were born with a *SILVER SPOON* in our mouths but we can pretend, can't we?"

CONTENTS

ACKNOWLEDGMENTS

CREATING *MODERN MIX* REQUIRED THE TIME, ENERGY AND DEDICATION OF MANY PEOPLE. I want to express my heartfelt gratitude to everyone who supported this project and encouraged me along the way:

To my partner and best friend from beginning to end, Jaithan Kochar, for his countless hours and witty words. Bonus points for his charisma, uniqueness, nerve and talent!

To my parents, Margie and Walter Roszkowski, for giving me a wonderful childhood and nurturing my creativity. To my grandparents Dottie and Eddie Novakowski, whom you will meet throughout this book. And to Jaithan's parents, Arvind and Mahendr Kochar, for their encouragement, advice and many take-home messages.

To my creative dream team: Bryan E. McCay, for his extraordinary pictures and untiring patience; Jessica Thomas, a.k.a. my Life Coach, who made magic on every page—a design superhero if there ever was one; Anna Ullman for her strokes of genius; Pauline Gallot for her illustrations; Michele Dubiel for running every shoot to the "peek" of perfection; Deanna Dewey for her creative input; Amy Troppmann and Jordan Perry for their stellar writing and research; and Austin Fremont for always making me laugh. Special thanks to Bunny Williams for introducing this book so generously and Elizabeth Blitzer for bringing us together.

To my longtime friends for standing by me through the years: Sue Scully, Hannah Gorman, Abby Jenkins, Dana Hendrickson, Tina Walsh, Jenny Holwill, Amy Goodwin, Ronnie Carroll, Samantha Emmerling, Phoebe Howard, Alex Heatly, Tori Mellott, Deborah Buck, Susan Lehman, Brendan Paul, Michelle Adams, Jackie Keber and Steve McKenzie.

To my colleagues and mentors: Gayle Butler, Kelly Kegans, and the team at *Better Homes & Gardens* for their unwavering support; Mary Emmerling for publishing my first styling byline; Wendy Waxman for giving me a chance; Senga Mortimer for showing me the golden ropes; and to Eric Pike, Margaret Russell and Newell Turner for their kindness and encouragement through the years.

To my longtime collaborators for their support: Jaclyn Pardini, Jan Jessup, Ken Weiner and Pamela Fleischer, Mollie Kitchens, Paul Romano, Beth Greene, Annie Selke, Robin Gordon, Robert Nachman, Anne Martin, Miry Park, Linda Wallace and Chris DeMeo.

To our publishing family at Gibbs Smith: Gibbs Smith, Suzanne Taylor, Melissa Dymock and especially to our editor Madge Baird, who nurtured this project from the start and, with fierce dedication, saw it through to the end. Special thanks to Kathryn M. Ireland for the introduction.

And to all my social media friends, thank you for inspiring me every day.

This compote is made from Paris Porcelain, one of my favorite types of ceramics. To learn more about the material, turn to page 49.

The barrel back chair I'm carrying in the photo on the back cover is one of a pair. I loved the feel of the original fabric, so I chose a similar print in fresh colors for the guest room in the city. The painting is by our good friend Mallory Page.

VOGUE LIVING HOUSES, GARDENS, PEOPLE

The Great American Pin-Up

BUNNIES Hunt Slonem

Eleanor Lambert: Still Here

An architectural painting that I found at a thrift shop in Palm Springs forms the backdrop to a vignette in our apartment, anchored by a simple arrangement of farm stand gladiolas. The console cabinet is mid-century from the Chelsea Flea Market in New York.

FOREWORD

WHEN I FIRST SAW THE IMAGES FROM EDDIE ROSS'S AMAZING BOOK *MODERN MIX*, I FELT I HAD MET MY ALTER EGO. For as long as I can remember, I have perused every antique store, thrift shop, tag sale and flea market looking for a treasure. Eddie has now captured the excitement of the "hunt" and presents his finds in one of the most beautiful books ever. Eddie takes the hunt to a new level.

If you want your home to have real personality, it will come from an assemblage of interesting objects and mementos. This book will help you focus on not only how to collect but also how to arrange things in stylish ways. Whether putting together a collection of colored glass, magnificent old silver or antique pieces of china, your eye will be trained by studying this book. You will learn that beautiful things are within your reach if you are willing to spend time hunting for those special objects.

The pictures in *Modern Mix* will help you arrange your finds with unique style. Mixing textures, shapes and colors is a real art, and Eddie shows how this is done. When objects are arranged well, they become still lifes in a room. Eddie also explores the art of entertaining and how special your table will look with your newfound treasures. Having beautiful glasses, china and linens is well within your reach. After studying this book, you will be inspired to shop tag sales, thrift shops and flea markets with a new eye.

I only hope I get there first.

Bunny Williams

Bunny Williams, Interior Designer

Late summer tree hydrangeas growing outside the kitchen window at Pine Hill Farm inspire a simple arrangement in an American art glass vase I found for $10 while antiquing in Omaha, NE.

I am not a wealthy man, but I know how they live.

My grandfather Eddie was the son of Polish immigrants; he met my grandmother Dottie at the Electrolux factory in Stamford, Connecticut, where they worked, and eventually they settled in Greenwich. My father, Walter, worked for the town, trimming trees and maintaining its parks; my mother, Margie, stayed at home, raising four boys almost entirely herself. While most of the other kids at school spoke of private planes and sleep-away camps, I enjoyed my summers in the garden helping my grandfather plant flowers, or in the kitchen with my mother making pierogi. We were a close-knit family, living under one roof, holding onto our Polish traditions.

In high school, I worked at a catering company washing dishes, scrubbing floors and taking out the trash. When the holidays came and we were short-staffed in the kitchen, I once arranged a crudité of vegetables on a grapevine sleigh with an eggplant sliced lengthwise and hollowed out for dip. It really wasn't any different from the flower arrangements I'd help my grandfather make growing up. Soon, I started working parties at grand estates, where I passed mini crab cakes on sterling silver trays and served Beluga caviar on mother-of-pearl spoons. As a caterer, I peered into the cabinets of magnificent kitchens, looking for a single pitcher, only to find a hundred. Big pitchers, little pitchers—porcelain, glass and silver. I opened drawers in butler's pantries with more serving pieces than Buckingham Palace. Long forks with four tines and short forks with two tines. Spoons with round bowls, oval bowls and spoons with teeth. There were toast racks and teapots, samovars and soup tureens, compotes and cake stands. China came with markings and linens with letters. Every piece had a story—a history—whether handed down or happened upon in some faraway place. Of course, I owned none of these things myself and would inherit little of the sort. But in the sublime beauty of coffee served delicately in a Herend Chinese Bouquet demitasse cup,

INSTAGRAM MOMENT: MY GRANDMOTHER, MOM-MOM, TAUGHT ME TO BE RESOURCEFUL. SHE BORROWED THE MINK STOLE AND HAD THIS RING ON LAYAWAY WHEN MY GRANDFATHER, POP-POP, SURPRISED HER WITH IT EARLY.

paired with a sterling silver Tiffany Audubon spoon, I glimpsed another kind of life.

Catering parties in Greenwich, I saw how the wealthy entertain. Styling homes for *House Beautiful*, I saw how they decorate. Oil paintings in living rooms hung splendidly over mantels flanked by cloisonné vases, Staffordshire dogs and Baccarat candlesticks. On bookcases and étagères, collections of blue-and-white porcelain punctuated stacks of beautiful books. Bar carts took center stage, stocked with silver cocktail shakers, gilded tumblers, and handblown glass decanters. Lacquered trays adorned coffee tables with Venetian glass bowls and vases filled with flowers. Boxes came in brass, shagreen, tortoiseshell and alabaster. Obelisks were made of marble, malachite, lapis and agate. Chinoiserie figurines rubbed elbows with African statues. Natural curiosities lent whimsy. Crystal added glamour. Everywhere I looked, captivating combinations of furniture, textiles, art and objects told deeply personal stories of who lived there, where they'd been and what they loved. In every treasure, trinket, knickknack and artifact, there was a life well lived—and I found it at the flea market. Not all of us were born with a silver spoon in our mouths, but we can pretend, can't we?

After graduating from the Culinary Institute of America, poring over every issue of *Martha Stewart Living* and eventually going to work at her test kitchens in Westport, I threw my first dinner party in a tiny studio apartment about the size of Martha's refrigerator. I pulled a card table up to a drop-leaf desk, covered it in an antique linen tablecloth and invited four guests to dine on wooden folding chairs I kept stashed beneath my twin-sized bed. On the desk I placed a glass flower frog from the hospital thrift shop with natural wood pencils and an English silver-plated toast rack with monogrammed stationery. A vintage gilt mirror hung over a whitewashed fireplace mantel, flanked by crystal wall sconces with a soft, flattering glow. For dinner, I served individual beef wellingtons, parisienne potatoes and roasted asparagus on gold-rimmed porcelain plates from an estate sale in Darien. Dessert came in the form of individual white chocolate soufflés in Limoges ramekins,

Clockwise from top: The greenhouse was always lush on the estate where I spent summers helping my grandfather root geraniums and coleuses, along with planting a variety of flowers and vegetables.

This floral chintz bedspread inspired by Dorothy Draper was the focal point in my grandparents' bedroom. Dottie used to love talking about its colors—pink, forest green and chocolate brown.

I was completely inspired by my new play kitchen one Christmas morning yet disappointed that the refrigerator wasn't cold and the water didn't run. But I sure did serve up some factory-fresh plastic veggies!

paired with a citrus crème anglaise in a footed crystal bowl from the Goodwill. At a Salvation Army, I'd found an English Sheffield silver sugar shaker, polished it to a shine and used it for powdered sugar on the table. When it came time for dessert, guests passed the shaker and crystal bowl from one to the other, sprinkling their soufflés and spooning crème anglaise with a sterling silver ladle engraved with an R monogram I'd found for $20 at a thrift shop in Westport. We may not have been in the library of a grand mansion in back country Greenwich, but huddled around my makeshift table on rickety wooden chairs, sipping coffee from demitasse cups with silver-plated spoons, we felt like royalty.

There isn't a school that will teach you how to create a rich, layered mix at home with castoffs you find at a flea market. There are no classes you can take on what to look for at a thrift shop to add Park Avenue flair to your parties. I learned about this stuff on the job—first, as a caterer and then as a style editor. Every French porcelain platter I picked up, every mid-century vase I filled with flowers, educated my eyes. In time, I started sharing what I'd learned with others, first in my column "Weekend Shopper" for *House Beautiful*, then on a blog I wrote with my partner Jaithan, in which we'd chronicle our decorating and entertaining experiences in the Hudson Valley. Soon, we began meeting our readers in

Pvt Edward J. Novakovich

ARMY LIFE

DOTTIE EVEN KEPT THE CARD FROM MY GREAT-GRANDPARENTS RIGHT IN THE BOX, ALONG WITH A COPY OF MY GRANDFATHER'S *ARMY LIFE* HANDBOOK.

WAR DEPARTMEN

Dottie also taught me that special things matter in a home. This Rogers Bros. silverware service in the Daffodil pattern was a wedding gift she used often before passing it on to me.

Sincerest wishes For everything

A Gift for the BRIDE

You now are hoping That life will bring!

AN ENTERTAINING LIFE

Tastes change along the journey into personal style, but every choice you make helps you grow. For years I've been using my finds to throw parties in even my tiniest apartments.

• *Top row:* Ironstone, glass and linen give my first grown-up buffet a country vibe. No, that's not my sister arranging hydrangeas in French porcelain baskets.

• *Middle row:* I rented a chafing dish for fondue, then filled in with fixings in punch bowls, compotes and celery vases. For a wedding, I decorated a frosted bakery cake with sugared fruits. When I hosted a dinner party, Dottie turned a fabric remnant into a table topper.

• *Bottom row:* At 15 I worked at a gourmet shop, Watson's, where I packaged individual pâtés with a spreader and crackers on decorative tiles. I was starting to hit my stride when I hosted this summer party with seafood and vegetables on ice in a vintage copper tray.

COUNTRY LIFE

Interview aug

INTERIOR·DESIGN

FLAIR

BETTER HOMES & GARDENS

House Beautiful

MAY

SPECTACULAR EXAMPLES OF
MAKEOVER MAGIC!
how to
change your
living space

VINTAGE DECORATING,
COOKING AND GARDENING
MAGAZINES ARE ENDLESS SOURCES
OF INSPIRATION TO CULTIVATE YOUR
STYLE. SHOP FLEA MARKETS, THRIFT
STORES AND EBAY FOR TITLES THAT
APPEAL TO YOU, THEN LOOK FOR NEW
WAYS TO INTERPRET OLD IDEAS.
SOMETHING MIGHT LOOK DATED AT
FIRST, BUT IT'S UP TO YOU TO
GIVE IT FRESH LIFE.

PALM BEACH ANNUAL

THE
ARCHITECTURAL
DIGEST

VOGUE

Color '77

SEPT.
$1

HOUSE
GARDEN

Letting go with color
The fabrics, the paint,
the plants, the art

AMERICANA
NUMBER

1950

EYES ON U.

Patterned sheets
What they do for your psyche

Medical breakthrough
Is American medicine
killing us?

Michel Guérard's
spectacular recipes from
Regine's new supper club

Gardening indoors
Raising spring bulbs in v
Decorating with plants

groups at flea markets across the country, where I would demystify the experience and teach them how to shop with confidence.

This book picks up where we left off, charting a colorful and exciting adventure into personal style. In each of the eight chapters—Inspire, Discover, Acquire, Restore, Curate, Mix, Style and Entertain—I share insights from my own journey, hoping to inspire yours. I decode the decorator mix you often see in "aspirational" homes and tell you how to do it on a real-life budget. Then I reveal my best-kept secrets to throwing fancy but friendly parties that will save you money and time. Everything you need to know to create a fresh, spirited look in your home that makes you happy, brings a smile to your family and entertains your guests in a way that feels authentic and expressive is here. The journey into personal style is rich with joy—and it begins now.

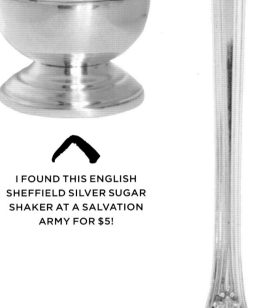

I FOUND THIS ENGLISH SHEFFIELD SILVER SUGAR SHAKER AT A SALVATION ARMY FOR $5!

THE TREASURE HUNT BEGINS

You don't have to spend a lot of money to live a beautiful life. I grew up humbly in one of the most affluent towns in America. Every weekend while working for a caterer, I'd go into beautiful homes to wash dishes that were more splendid than I'd ever imagined. Then I started looking in flea markets, thrift shops and tag sales to find items at prices I could afford. I bought these pieces to serve dessert at my very first dinner party. Even now, years later, I'll pass around the crystal bowl or the sterling silver ladle I found at thrift shops around the corner from those houses that I worked in and feel like the richest man in town.

FIND INSPIRATION ANYWHERE

You don't have to look far to find things that can inspire your creativity. After a trip to the flea market, a farm stand or even just a walk in the woods, I always return home with fresh ideas for new projects. *Clockwise from top left:*

• Colorful French Bakelite flatware can inspire everything from the table design to the dessert you serve.

• Whimsical, vintage ceramic chess pieces create conversation on a bookcase.

• Take a cue from your closet, combining colors and patterns in a room the way you would an outfit.

• Hand-decorated chinoiserie plates collected over time become a unique set.

• Vintage textiles can easily inspire new projects. This one I might use to cover a small chair, make a roman shade or sew into a table topper.

• I'm always buying vintage decorating, gardening and table setting books that inspire me. It's fun to see how points of view on such topics evolve over time.

• Fresh-cut flowers from the garden or even carnations from a grocery store can create simple, beautiful arrangements.

This big brass tray might have lost its mid-century table base, but that didn't stop me from paying $50 for it at a flea market. Hand-etched Moroccan motifs give it a worldly look that feels right at home on my dining table topped with potted orchids and plants.

EDUCATE your eyes and the world will come into *FOCUS.*

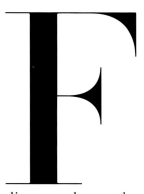or as long as I can remember, I've chased the exhilarating thrill of discovery. From an under-the-radar restaurant to an over-the-top chintz, I'm always on the lookout for what's new, what's old, what's hot, what's not, what everybody's talking about on Instagram and what nobody yet knows.

Of all the many things I've discovered over the years, an understanding of taste—that curious bundle of style, selection and sensitivity—changed me for life. I was at culinary school in upstate New York, learning one definition of the word and catering parties on weekends in tony suburbs in Connecticut when I learned the other: Taste, it seemed, wasn't just about creating dishes that had to be perfectly seasoned; it was about how you chose to live and all of the perfect imperfections that went along with it.

While catering parties in school, I learned that taste is everywhere in a home. It starts with the hardware on a front door, adds color to an entryway and illuminates the kitchen. It hangs from windows in a dining room, enlivens the walls with pattern and adds texture underfoot. It even finds its way onto the table, into the flowers and down to the napkins. In every detail of those sprawling houses, a homeowner's taste (or their decorator's) influenced them all. Anyone can have taste, I thought, but good taste? That was expensive.

Then I discovered the flea market and the world opened up. Suddenly, good taste didn't seem so out of reach. If I knew what to look for—the objects, materials and marks that surrounded me at all of those parties—I could go to a thrift shop or stop at a yard sale for the very same things at prices I could afford. From that moment on, I studied the marks on china, silver, linens and glass. I picked up anything and everything, examining its color, shape and texture, the feel of its weight in my hands, then set out to find it all for myself. Ten dollars an hour may not seem like much now, but it bought a lot of dishes at the flea market!

Years later, I discovered the high-end decorating

INSTAGRAM MOMENT: I WAS PACKING UP AFTER A TRIP TO BRIMFIELD WHEN I SNAPPED THIS PICTURE OF MY FINDS, WHICH INCLUDE TREASURES IN GLASS, BRASS, PORCELAIN AND GOLD PLATE.

world and an entirely new level of taste. I was working at a magazine called *Classic American Home* when my boss summoned me into her office and told me to go to the D&D, please, for petit point fabrics and make it fast. As a newbie editor in New York still unfamiliar with the Design & Decoration Building, where, among other things, petit point fabrics are sampled and sold, I didn't have a clue what she was talking about. These days, a couple of clicks on my phone could have sent me on my way, but this was the sort of pre-Googlian panic that could have ruptured a blood vessel. Eventually I figured it out, and when I did, the world opened up yet again.

Sourcing high-end products for stories in magazines, and styling for photography homes by accomplished decorators with the most refined taste, I've seen and touched firsthand some of the best, most beautiful things for the home. They're out there in the world in places that are closer than you might think for every one of us to discover. You just have to know where to start.

In this chapter you'll discover the colors, textures and finishes of some of my favorite materials. There's the acid yellow splash of a cased glass candy dish, the shimmering warmth of a prized copper pot and the homespun chic of an embroidered bedspread. You'll also brush up on history with intriguing facts about how and when these materials were first developed. Of course, there are separate volumes dedicated to each, but I share the ones that I love and collect, hoping to spark in you the curiosity for more.

Most of the items here are smaller in size, made from materials commonly found at flea markets, thrift shops and yard sales. But that doesn't mean they're not special! I once found a set of 12 dinner knives with mother-of-pearl handles at a Salvation Army in perfect condition. If you know what to look for, you can find it just about anywhere. Educate your eyes, and the world will come into focus.

Taste, I've come to learn, changes with every experience, every person, place and thing you encounter in the world. Good taste, whatever it looks like, is about living with the things you love and trusting that they go together. Good taste is a journey into personal style that begins with discovery.

DISCOVER *GLASS*

Add beauty and utility to your home with shimmering glassware.

You would be hard-pressed to find a plastic drinking glass in my cupboards. I'd rather take a few minutes to wash something that's beautiful than buy a synthetic version and send it to a landfill. Glassmaking is an ancient art, so as tastes change and technology advances, some types fall out of fashion or become obsolete, turning up in places for you to discover all over again. There are many ways that glassware can add

radiant style throughout your house. For instance, serve a delicious summer salad on a chilled glass plate. Replace a plastic mouthwash bottle with a handsome Venetian glass decanter. Group a collection of vintage bottles filled with hyacinths, tulips and daffodils on the fireplace mantel. Or put a Duncan Heinz cake on a pressed glass cake pedestal in a pattern you love. Gorgeous glassware can even make unloading the dishwasher feel like you're living every day in style.

Adding metal compounds to glass creates a kaleidoscope of colors. Gold gives it a ruby-red hue; cadmium makes it yellow; and manganese in old bottles turns them purple in the sun. This is a selection of my colorful glassware, ranging from handblown 1800s crystal to machine-made stemware by CB2.

GLASS CLASS

New discoveries in glass manufacturing have resulted in multiple techniques. To produce handblown pieces, molten glass is collected on the end of a metal pipe, inflated with air and worked into a desired shape. Mold-blown glass starts off the same way but is blown into a mold to assume its shape and pattern. Commercial pressing machines automate the process, producing pressed, or patterned, glass for everyday use. Here are some of my favorite glass types to look for in your search.

LOOK FOR CZECH AND BOHEMIAN FLASHED GLASSWARE IN GEMSTONE HUES. ITEMS BROUGHT BACK AS SOUVENIRS OFTEN TURN UP AT THRIFT SHOPS AND TAG SALES.

BOHEMIAN *Once part of the Czech Republic, Bohemia is known for its makers of high-quality crystal and glassware. To create this two-toned effect, an artisan flashed a thin layer of ruby-red glass over a layer of clear, and then hand cut and engraved the piece.*

STERLING OVERLAY *I've been mad for mid-century artist Dorothy Thorpe's designs since long before the boys on* Mad Men *started swilling Scotch in her Roly Poly glasses with sterling silver bands. She also applied it to textured crystal in artful brushstroke patterns.*

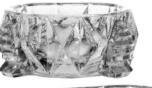

DEPRESSION *To perk people up during the '30s, glassmakers in the Midwest mass-produced colorful pressed glass pieces that were made for everyday use and would be free gifts with purchase at grocery stores.*

OPALINE *Made only in France until 1890, true opaline has a translucent appearance that comes in many colors; pink, white and yellow are my favorites. Beware of fakes, as some dealers try to pass off milk glass at opaline prices.*

MILK *The Italians invented this glass, named for the milky white color, but it was also made in pink, blue, black and other colors. I spotted this Oriental Empress vase at the Fenton Museum and found one on eBay.*

A CUT ABOVE

Crystal is a heavier but thinner type of glass that contains lead, which softens the material for decorative glasswork like cutting and copper-wheel hand engraving. Strike a piece of crystal and it will produce a "ping." Hold it up to the sun and it will sparkle brilliantly. The large crystal bowl with a gilded edge was gifted to me after I pointed it out to a group of blog readers at the Metrolina Vintage & Antique Show in Charlotte, North Carolina. A modern floral pattern gives the bowl a chic, ethereal quality.

AMERICAN GLASS MAKERS

At one point in time, the Untied States had over 500 glass companies. Now you can practically count them on two hands. Since this glass was made here, secondhand markets are full of beautiful stemware, serving pieces and decorative accessories in more colors than the rainbow. Here are a few of my favorite manufacturers and tips on how to identify them.

- **HEISEY GLASS** Newark, Ohio, was pressed in clear and vivid colors. Look for a capital H in a diamond shape on the bottom of the piece. My favorite pattern is the clear Greek key.

- **ANCHOR HOCKING** Lancaster, Ohio, was best known for Fire-King, introduced in the 1940s. Jadeite was a pretty green, but I collect azurite, a beautiful light blue glass with clean lines.

- **WESTMORELAND** Grapeville, Pennsylvania, made high-quality, whitest of the white milk glass, from compotes to cake pedestals. Look for the WM marking pressed into the glass.

- **IMPERIAL** Bellaire, Ohio, is best known for Carnival glass they produced in marigold. But my favorite is the Candlewick pattern in clear, with a simple beaded edge that works with everything.

- **FOSTORIA** Moundsville, West Virginia, was best known for its American pattern. It's clear in color with a geometric pattern reminiscent of a quilt. You can't go wrong with this iconic pattern.

- **CORNING** Corning, New York, made very sturdy and strong glass suitable for use from the home to the science lab. I love the modern-shaped pitchers, canisters and lab-ware.

MURANO A crimped edge turned this piece into a convenient ashtray; it was caked in nicotine soot when I found it a thrift shop. Air bubbles were a common technique developed by Murano glassmakers, giving movement to their designs.

MERCURY I love the mirrorlike finish on mercury-glass lamps, vases and gazing balls from the 1800s, mold-blown into double-walled shapes and coated on the inside with silver nitrate inserted through a small hole and sealed with a plug.

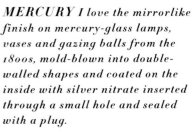

BRISTOL I have vases in pink, white, clam-broth gray and this vivid turquoise, many of them hand decorated with cheery scenes of flowers and foliage.

VENETIAN I use this over-the-top pitcher to serve after-dinner drinks like cordials and liqueurs. Its exuberant shape and finely twisted handle add European élan to clean-lined companions.

LOOK FOR CASED-GLASS VASES, GOBLETS, DISHES AND DECANTERS IN VIBRANT HUES LIKE MARINE BLUE, ACID YELLOW AND POPSICLE RED. PAIR THEM WITH MORE TRADITIONAL STYLES LIKE CUT CRYSTAL FOR A MODERN MIX.

When it comes to colorful glassware, don't just make a statement. Make an *EXCLAMATION POINT!*

This dish and the green pitcher, opposite, get their eye-candy color from layers of opaque white and colored glass that have been blown and fused together. Italian and Scandinavian cased glass are the ones that I prize the most.

GLASS ACT

Colorful glasses are the first things I look for at any Goodwill. I like the light-as-a-feather types with ultra-thin glass and graceful silhouettes. Vintage or new, they come in a range of styles, sizes and shapes, and every one of them adds personality to the party! There's the blushing swirl of a cranberry pink coupe, serving up Prosecco and getting frisky with the servers. CB2's Marta makes a citrus green splash, while an amber cordial glass sits brooding by the fire. Goblets in cobalt are full of fizzy Perrier, nursing a hangover from last night's Cabernet. Cruella looks the serious type, but pour her something fruity like a mango margarita, and she'll light up the room with a sour-sweet chic. And even if Boozy Suzy breaks another glass, don't let it bring you down—a replacement is often just a click away.

I USE THIS PRESSED-GLASS DECANTER IN A DIAMOND-POINT PATTERN TO SERVE CRÈME DE CASSIS FOR CHAMPAGNE COCKTAILS. THE TURQUOISE COUPES ARE BY PORTIEUX VALLERYSTHAL.

DISCOVER *METALS*

Every metal has its own personality. Choose the types that suit your style.

I was driving by a tag sale once, slowed down for a scan and practically leapt out the window trying to nab a set of Mauviel copper pots. New ones are expensive, and these were barely used. The homeowner told me they were a wedding gift; she just couldn't be bothered to polish them. Another time I was shopping an estate sale and there was a gorgeous, old sideboard in the dining room. When I opened it up, I couldn't believe what I saw: inside one of the drawers I found a sterling silver butter knife with an engraved *Ross* on the handle (page 39)! The types of metal you're likely to come across in tableware and other objects vary in color, sheen and warmth, so every one of them can add something unique to your home.

LOOK FOR VINTAGE METAL TABLEWARE IN SIMPLE SHAPES. EARLY OBJECTS WERE OFTEN THE MOST BASIC, WITH A PRIMITIVE CHARM THAT PAIRS WELL WITH MORE ELABORATE PIECES TO CREATE A MODERN MIX. FOR AN AUTUMN DINNER, I'LL FILL THIS PEWTER SPOON FROM THE GOODWILL—SALT ON ONE SIDE, PEPPER ON THE OTHER—THEN PUT A LITTLE SPOON IN IT AND PASS IT AROUND THE TABLE.

My arsenal of metal includes a crimped copper dish, a brass bud vase, a silver-plated platter, a pewter serving spoon and a cast brass dish in the shape of a fig leaf by Oscar Hansen for Virginia Metalcrafters.

METAL COUNT

From serving pieces to accessories, you'll find objects in a variety of beautiful metals, and each one of them brings a distinct mood, a mind-set, a personality to a home. Stainless steel is casual or sleek; pewter brings an old-world feel; copper and brass add warmth; and gold is straight up rich. Here are a few of my favorite metals, marks and finishes to inspire your search.

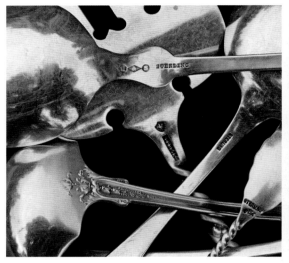

PEWTER *Too much pewter in one place goes Ye Olde Colonial faster than you can shout "The British are coming!" But when the weather turns chill, large pieces of serveware, such as platters, pitchers and compotes, add charm to table settings and buffets.*

BRASS *Although brass might be a poor man's gold, it has a rich gleam that's turning up in everything from candlesticks to cutlery. Unlacquered brass mellows to a dull finish; I prefer all my brass pieces polished to a high shine for a modern look.*

STERLING SILVER *It's the whitest, most lustrous precious metal. Pieces are often marked with 925 for a minimum of 92.5% pure silver content. For decades, sterling silver was de rigueur for dinner, adorning formal tables with flatware, serving pieces and accessories.*

DIRILYTE *The Dirilyte Company began business as Dirigold in 1924, but there isn't an ounce of gold in it; a bronze alloy gives Dirilyte its golden hue. Of the four flatware patterns the company produced, Regal has the cleanest lines that mix in easily on any table.*

COPPER *Nothing beats copper's conductivity for cooking (thank you, Julia Child) or the warmth it adds to a kitchen. Shop flea markets for heavy pieces with a thick layer of copper, inscribed numbers, dovetailed seams and handmade rivets holding the handles in place.*

GOLD PLATE *Even if it's just pizza night, I'll pull out the gold plate for a little extra glitz with my pepperoni. There's only a thin layer of gold over another metal like silver or steel, so it's still affordable. Channel your inner Donatella, darling, but tread lightly— less is more.*

BLUE STEEL

Sterling shouldn't steal the show. I prize some of my stainless pieces just as much as I do any other metal. My favorites are mid-century modern from Denmark and Japan. Sleek shapes and mixed materials give them an edge over their newer counterparts. The serving pieces are Danish; the saltcellars, footed dish and flatware with composite handles are Japanese.

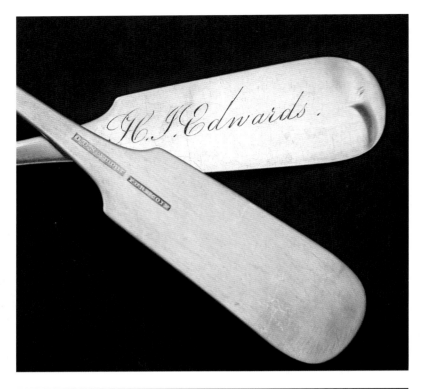

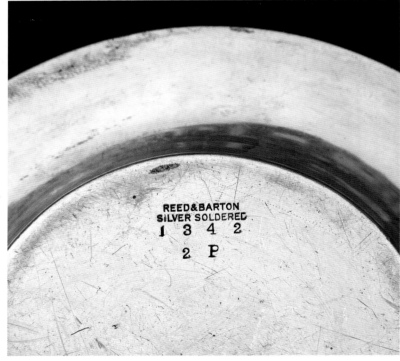

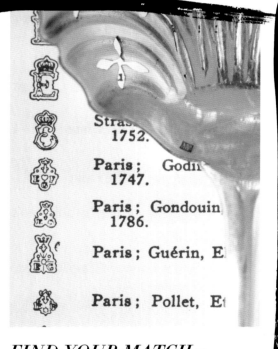

SILVER LININGS

While silver objects vary in value depending on their purity, I look for styles that work together. Sterling is the purest, but plating objects with silver over other metals reduces the price. *Top right:* Silver plate traces roots to Sheffield, England, in 1743; later wares were often marked E.P.N.S., for electroplated nickel silver. *Top left:* Early Americans took their hard-earned coins in a mishmash of metals to silversmiths, who melted down and molded the material into featherlight flatware. Look for serving pieces with monograms to add southern charm to a buffet. *Bottom left:* Tiffany is the silver standard for American manufacturing, but my other flea market favorites are Gorham, Wallace, Reed & Barton and Rogers Brothers.

FIND YOUR MATCH There are volumes of books on silver markings that can tell you where and when a piece was made. Whenever I'm matching up a new serving piece or a set of forks I have found, I feel like Ralphie in *The Christmas Story* using my secret decoder pin to decipher the fate of the planet. I once found a fantastic ladle at the bottom of a box of tarnished silver and it turned out to be Christofle. Here's hoping your markings are more French sterling than Ovaltine!

I SCORED THIS
STERLING SILVER
BUTTER KNIFE AT
AN ESTATE SALE IN
OAKLAND, CALIFORNIA
WITH OUR FRIEND
TERRI OF THE BLOG
LA DOLFINA. IT'S
PATENTED 1878 WITH
A HAND-ENGRAVED
ROSS.

*I love an elaborate
monogram or a coat of
arms on old silver, even if
they're not my own. Hand
engravings enrich a table
with history, conjuring
images of landed aristocrats
in country castles and
knights in shining armor.*

DISCOVER *TEXTILES*

Transform any room or table setting with colorful fabrics and vintage linens.

I was living in a tiny studio apartment when I began collecting linens; they practically took up no space. I'd soak them in my itty-bitty kitchen and dry them on the fire escape. Then I'd use a mix of antique pillowcases on my bed, monogrammed hand towels in my bathroom and damask napkins on a folding table for dinner parties. Later I started buying remnants of beautiful fabric at estate sales—you don't need large quantities. For instance, you can take two yards of fabric from an outlet store and turn it into pillows or staple it over an upholstered headboard. There are lots of different textiles out there that can make an impact wherever you choose to use them.

Decorative handwork including fringe, embroidery and appliqué embellishes a collection of my sherbet-hued linens spanning more than a hundred years. White can be trite, so to update the napkins with a monogrammed B, I dipped them in Rit dye for a fresh look.

LOOK FOR VINTAGE LINENS WITH MODERN MOTIFS. THE PINK LINEN NAPKINS APPLIQUÉD WITH A GREEK KEY BORDER WERE A GIFT FROM A BLOG READER. I ONCE PAIRED THEM WITH A PINK OMBRE CAKE FOR A BIRTHDAY PARTY.

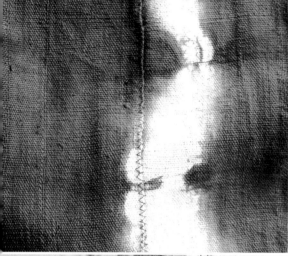

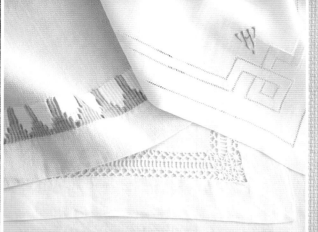

COMMON THREADS

Discover my favorite types of vintage textiles and the techniques used to create and decorate them. *Clockwise from top left:*

- **TIE-DYE** Traces its roots to Africa, where for centuries natural dyes have been used to create worldly prints.

- **DRAWNWORK** Created by removing threads from a fabric's weave to form lacelike patterns.

- **EMBROIDERY** This cross-stitched bedspread was part of Jaithan's mother's trousseau.

- **FRINGE** Brush fringe can feel formal, while washed fringe can feel casual.

- **SHIBORI** Created using Japanese tie-dyeing techniques. It's always in style.

- **DOILIES** A graphic square one paired with a pink lacquered bar tray is very chic.

- **COLORFUL MONOGRAMS** Like vintage graffiti with heirloom appeal.

- **SCALLOPS** Lend a pretty touch when paired with a hard edge.

- **CHINTZ** Glazed cotton with a shiny finish often printed with large bright florals.

- **APPLIQUÉ** Timeless chic in tonal palettes.

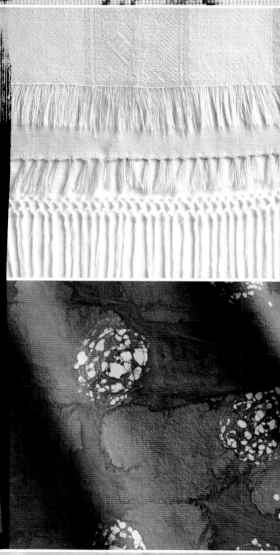

An *OPULENT MONOGRAM* on fine linen napkins might not be yours, but you're still part of the family.

QUEEN BEE

Ancient royals used monograms to communicate power in every language. Upwardly mobile Westerners in the 1800s used them as status symbols, adorning personal belongings with letters in sinuous combinations. I'm always on the lookout for vintage linens with stylish or humorous monograms. I have hand towels embroidered with OCD that always garner a laugh from guests.

DISCOVER *CERAMICS*

Bring beauty to your table and beyond with ceramic wares.

For centuries, craftsmen have been turning fired clay into ceramic objects. Some were purely decorative; others had specific uses. Over time, developments in manufacturing led to mass-produced tableware. Since ceramics are durable, you can find an endless variety of types, shapes and patterns on the secondary market. New pieces, whether manufactured or handmade, can add just as much personality to your table. But ceramic's beauty extends beyond dishes. Pick up a vintage ginger jar lamp in a colorful glaze from a tag sale and freshen it up with a new shade. Or find a set of old tiles at a flea market and install them on a fireplace surround. There are many types of ceramic serveware and accessories for the home; these are a few of my favorite.

Nemadji pottery was once thought to be crafted by Native Americans—a myth its Minnesota manufacturer chose, strategically, not to contest. I found this marbleized vase at an antique mall in Denver; a quick dip into a vat of vinegar, water and paint produced its vivid, swirling surface.

On a slim console in our apartment, I display a variety of ceramic objects, including a Paris Porcelain pitcher and plate, a matte art pottery vase, a tea cup by Dorothy Thorpe and a whimsical candlestick by Fitz and Floyd.

MAKERS & MARKS

Years ago, when a famous potter signed his wares, it was something akin to Picasso signing a painting. If you're trying to complete a set of china, knowing the manufacturer and pattern is important. But even if you don't, companies like Replacements, Ltd. will help you do the research. Personally, I try to look beyond the mark. Just because it's "good" doesn't mean it works for you. Once, I scored a deal on a set of eight Wedgwood dinner plates in a turquoise and gray floral; the colors were pretty enough, but I just never grew to like the pattern—even though it was a great price on a high-end set. My advice? Pay attention to marks, but fall for colors and patterns that speak to you. They're the true makings of your modern mix.

G. L. ASHWORTH & BROTHERS LTD. *By hand-painting colorful enamels on top of a one-color transfer print, manufacturers like Ashworth were able to add a finer touch to mass-produced pieces like this ironstone vegetable dish I found at a flea market.*

GEORGES BRIARD *The jade-colored Imperial Malachite is mid-century designer Georges Briard's most popular pattern. Printed decals were transferred to the surface of this shallow soup bowl and accented with gold.*

A. G. NINER *If the mark on a piece doesn't ring familiar and you can't find any further clues about the pattern, it likely bears the name of a bygone fine goods shop, like A. G. Niner in London, that produced it as a one-off commission.*

COALPORT *I used to see Coalport all the time on dishes I washed catering parties. So when I found a set of 12 of these hand-painted dinner plates at a flea market, I knew they were worth the $300 asking price.*

LENOX *Creators of the first North American bone china to be used in the White House, Lenox has the honor of having made tableware for six U.S. presidents. This Lenox marking was used only between 1906 and 1930.*

SPODE *Transferware is like a permanent peel 'n' stick tattoo for china without the stinging prices of hand-painted wares. English potter Josiah Spode famously developed the technique in the 1780s. Artwork is engraved onto a copper plate, inked, printed on paper and transferred to a ceramic surface. Spode remains among the most prestigious manufacturers today.*

NEOCLASSICAL GRANDEUR

Josiah Wedgwood was the Steve Jobs of stoneware. Since 1759, the English pottery firm he founded has been producing some of the most innovative and ethereal ceramics of all time. Jasperware, Wedgwood's most famous pottery, is also one of my favorites. You can easily recognize its relief decorations on matte stoneware bodies, like hand-carved cameos. Pale blue is the most common color, but I prefer the pink, lavender, sage green and black decorated with neoclassical motifs, *above.* The ashtray, *above right,* which was a gift from Jaithan, is a commemorative piece marking the coronation of Queen Elizabeth II, though I'm content to use it as a catchall and pretend it was monogrammed just for me. Wedgwood's black basalt also broke new ground: the pottery's obsidian bodies were made of a reddish-brown clay that turned black in firing. The new teacup and saucer set, *right,* is shaped simply but looks ultra-luxe rendered in matte black with soft gloss interiors.

LOOK FOR SHADOWS OF YOUR FINGERS WHEN YOU HOLD UP PORCELAIN TO THE LIGHT. IT'S FIRED AT HIGHER TEMPERATURES THAN OTHER CERAMIC WARES, FORMING A GLASSLIKE MATERIAL THAT'S THIN, STRONG AND TRANSLUCENT.

OLD PARIS

Paris Porcelain (or "Old Paris" Porcelain) was made in France from the late 1700s to 1870. I stock up whenever and wherever I find plates in the Wedding Band pattern embellished with simple gold rings. It's like the classic white Oxford of entertaining that mixes easily on any table.

DISCOVER *PLASTICS*

Replicate exotic materials or add futuristic chic to your space.

Not every plastic on the market is a poly something-or-other molded into things like peanut butter jars or plastic cutlery and cups. The disposable stuff has its place, but when it comes to curating style at home, there are only a handful of specific plastics I look for. The earlier ones replicate expensive and exotic materials such as ivory, horn, bone and wood. More recent plastics, like Lucite and acrylic, are transparent wonders that can update a room in an instant. Introduce plastics sparingly and combine them with richer, more organic materials for a modern mix.

Though this wall bracket looks like carved giltwood, it's actually an injection-molded plastic in the manner of a fancy Italian antique for a fraction of the cost. Beginning in the 1960s, American companies like Syroco and Burwood mass-produced clocks, plaques, mirrors and other wall art in glitzy styles, including Regency and Rococo.

CLEAR STORY

Lucite (or Perspex or Plexiglas) is the clear-cut choice to update just about anything. Pair a Plexiglas coffee table with a camelback sofa, acrylic knobs with a traditional dresser, Lucite rings with damask napkins. Dorothy Thorpe twisted Lucite into pretzel-like candlesticks. Shop thrift stores and online for Lucite objects of the sort pictured here, but steer clear of anything cracked or yellowing. Candles like these are often flecked with silver and gold; you can't burn them, but they're an easy way to update traditional candlesticks. New items from big-box stores can be just as chic.

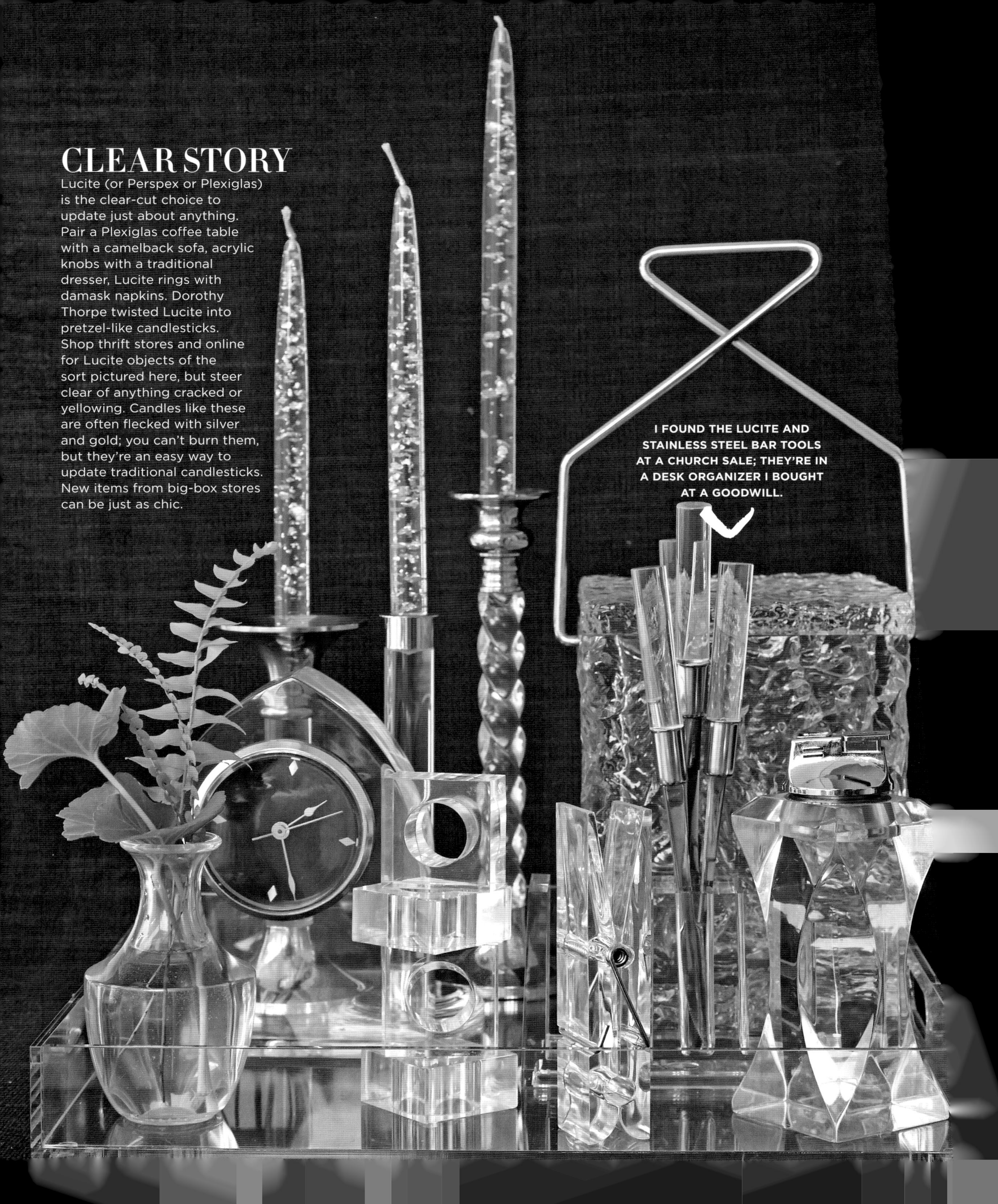

I FOUND THE LUCITE AND STAINLESS STEEL BAR TOOLS AT A CHURCH SALE; THEY'RE IN A DESK ORGANIZER I BOUGHT AT A GOODWILL.

GIVE IT A REST To fashion a set of knife rests with see-through appeal, ask your local plastics shop to cut a twisted Lucite rod into two-inch segments, then use an acrylic glue to attach ready-made cubes at both ends. Tap and Canal Plastics are two of my favorite sources online.

LOOK FOR FRENCH IVORY CARVING SETS. THEY ADD CHIVALRY TO A BANQUET OR A BARBECUE. A KITCHEN SHOP CAN SHARPEN THE BLADE OR REPLACE IT ALTOGETHER.

FAUX REAL

Most of the celluloid in my closets is French ivory, an early plastic dating to the 1870s, with the color, weight and smoothness of natural ivory. Fashionable Victorians favored it for the handles of serving pieces and flatware, *right,* adorning tables with a splendid array of utensils for every course. Fish knives and forks, often with sterling silver ferrules and engraved blades, were a popular choice; spoons were rarer. French ivory yellows with age—a perfect pairing for china with amber hues. The material was also molded into affordable mirrors, brushes and manicure tools, *above;* genteel types used them for primping at dressing tables. I'll still use a round pillbox for stashing paper clips on a desk or a clean-lined brush for sprucing up suede shoes.

KITCHEN JEWELS

Bakelite is another early plastic developed in Connecticut. Promoted in the 1930s as "jewels for the kitchen," serving pieces and flatware with Bakelite handles came in many colors; rare varieties were two-toned with geometric patterns in red or black with cream. For a more versatile look, I'll put together pieces from my collection in the warmer palette, *opposite.* The ochre, butterscotch and burnt sienna hues pair beautifully with simple egg dishes at a weekend brunch.

DISCOVER *NATURALS*

Bring nature home with organic elements and motifs.

Natural specimens in a room are sculptural and surprising. As a child, I often accompanied my grandfather to a tiny stretch of beach on the Long Island Sound where I'd gather up sea glass in lavender, jade and aqua, filling jars on my desk with their frosty light. Living with natural elements ties us to life itself, and it needn't be costly or time-consuming to find things that inspire you. Some of the most organic objects in a room are often the most intriguing.

2-D representations of natural motifs are another way to bring nature home. The tortoise shell print wrapping paper is from Caspari. Look for other patterned papers in faux croc and marble, then use them to decoupage a modern tray.

THE
GARDEN
AND ITS
ACCESSORIES

LORING
UNDERWOOD

HOW TO
KNOW
THE
WILD
FLOWERS

DANA

ANIMALS AND MINERALS

Unearth natural beauty with any of these fine specimens. *Clockwise from top left:*

- **ALABASTER** Evokes classic Italian chic. Look for boxes, vases and compotes.

- **HORN** Infuses instant warmth. A set of mini spoons is fun for desserts or hors d'oeuvres.

- **ABALONE** Iridescent insides of abalone shells add glam as boxes, bowls and sculptures.

- **ONYX** Edgy and exotic in candlesticks, bookends and occasional table tops.

- **ANTLER** Juxtapose furniture and lighting with sleeker counterparts for a modern mix.

- **TORTOISE** Lends a preppy note. If you find an affordable vintage, faux or 2-D piece, buy it.

- **LEATHER** Conjures English club in classic colors. Opening bills isn't so bad with a brass and lizard letter opener scored at a thrift shop.

- **AMETHYST** Polished stone gives hard-edged glamour to lighting, boxes, bookends and coasters.

- **MOTHER-OF-PEARL** Turns an inexpensive caviar into a Russian czar's dream.

- **MALACHITE** Fits in anywhere, like greenery.

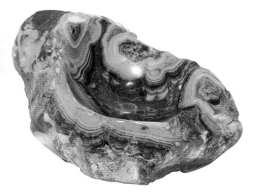

NATURE TRAIL

Here are my favorite woody materials, tones and textures. *Clockwise from top left:*

• **CORK** Lends earthy texture to lamps, apothecary jars and kitchen equipment, like this graphic trivet.

• **TEAK** Brings Danish modern style to any room. Look for furniture, trays, breadboards, ice buckets, salad bowls and serving utensils.

• **STAG HORN** Flatware and carving sets give tables and buffets Aspen-chalet chic.

• **FIGURAL** Adds humor, like this trivet fish our friend Jessica caught for us.

• **TIGER MAPLE** Looks handsome and exotic in mortars and pestles, vases and candlesticks.

• **STRAW** Feels like summer. Think cocktails on the porch, tableware, trays, placemats and baskets.

• **HAND-CARVED** Imparts primitive charm. Look for unusual objects or serving pieces hand crafted by artisans.

• **BAMBOO** Evokes a West Indies vibe in its natural state. Faux bamboo has been a decorator go-to for decades.

• **GRAPEVINE** Adds a gnarly note wherever it goes. The French favor it for wine and cheese.

HIGH TIDE

Ever the lavish lot, Victorians in 19th-century England dined at sumptuous tables with specialized serving pieces for each dish, many with mother-of-pearl handles. Reinvent antiques for modern meals. For instance, use round, flat spoons for Caprese salads, forks with twin tines for spearing olives and pierced spoons for dusting powdered sugar on desserts. You can also find new mother-of-pearl spoons made for caviar, then use them for serving individual hors d'oeuvres. This collection was amassed over fifteen years.

You never know what *TREASURE* you'll find when you take the time to look!

Roll up your sleeves and get ready to dig! Hidden gems await in all of the bins and boxes at flea markets most others pass up. Now that you've discovered some of the materials, makers and marks to look for, the treasure hunt begins.

I started digging for treasure the old-fashioned way. Every day after school, my friend Brian and I would ride our bikes to the woods behind old houses in Glenville to go bottle-digging in areas where the town's early residents once discarded their household waste. With a pair of shovels, a pitchfork and gardening tools, we unearthed the most beautiful glass bottles in every size, shape and color. Coca-Cola bottles came in clear and green glass; Pond's jars were a milky white; and medical elixir bottles displayed the names of neighboring cities—Stamford, Port Chester and Rye—where they were made.

Of all of the bottles we found, my favorite was a deep cobalt blue embossed with Bromo-Seltzer in thick block letters. After removing layers of dirt and leaves, I gave the bottle a thorough rinse, filled it with paint brushes and placed it on a rolltop desk my grandfather had made for me to do craft projects. Gazing up at its hue, the way the letters caught the light, I thought I'd uncovered the most brilliant sapphire in the world. I loved that little bottle and couldn't imagine why anyone would have thrown it away.

After culinary school, I set about furnishing my first grown-up apartment, a 325-square-foot studio in Greenwich on the town's main thoroughfare. By then I had graduated from digging through the detritus of the past in the forest to the flea market, where I found a growing collection of antique ironstone and silver-plated serving pieces, which I kept in an antique pharmaceutical cabinet that my grandfather had stripped of peeling paint to reveal shelves lined in zinc. From my grandmother, I received a prized peacock blue lamp with a chinoiserie cameo on its base. It was a magnificent lamp, and as much as Dottie loved it herself, she knew I loved it even more.

To find more furniture at affordable prices, I began my search at the Knights of Columbus Flea Market, where I scored a 1940s French upholstered chair in a navy velvet stripe, a white ginger jar lamp and two wooden side tables—one round, the other rectangular—with drawers for added storage. I spray-painted each of them a glossy black and picked up two new

INSTAGRAM MOMENT: WHEN I DID A TAG SALE OF MY OWN, I STACKED BENCHES ON TABLES TO CREATE LEVELS, THEN GROUPED SIMILAR OBJECTS TO MAKE IT EASIER FOR SHOPPERS TO FIND WHAT THEY LIKE.

lamp shades to tie the two together. At tag sales in backcountry Greenwich, I sifted through the unwanted belongings of my well-to-do neighbors, snapping up candlesticks, cookware and art of every kind which I hung in precarious groupings from floor to ceiling. On a routine spin through the hospital thrift shop, I found four custom curtain panels in an ivory and green damask with tassel trim and hand-finished hems—a couture casualty, I imagined, of one of the town's fabled wars of the roses. And finally, in the attic of a house in Darien, minutes before the end of the day's sale, I found a graphic flat-weave rug from the 1980s in every color of the apartment.

Pulling the room together, assembling all of the bits I had inherited or happened upon, never did I manage to find a sofa that worked. They were either too big or too small, too simple or too elaborate. Whenever friends dropped by, I always had plenty of saltcellars on hand, but no sofa! Finally I found one I loved at a Salvation Army. It was just the right size with a great shape, loose cushions and rolled arms. Polaroid in hand, I stopped in to an upholsterer and nearly keeled over at the cost: to repair the frame, add new fill and upholster the piece, he estimated $1,100—and that didn't even include the 20 yards of fabric! It was an astonishing amount of money that I couldn't afford, but at the same time, now I knew exactly the type of sofa I was looking for and found a new version, customizing it the way I wanted—navy blue with flax piping—for a fraction of the cost.

Over the years, I've learned that as much as you might love digging in flea markets and yard sales for special pieces with one-of-a-kind charm, sometimes it makes more sense to buy new. From online retailers to corner thrift stores, there are so many places to find stylish things for your home, it can easily be overwhelming where to look. There are places to fit everyone's budget, but you're going to have to work harder, dig deeper to score a deal. Now that you've discovered several things to look for—the materials, makers and marks that start to shape your personal style—you can acquire them more quickly and affordably if you know where to look.

Just don't forget your shovel.

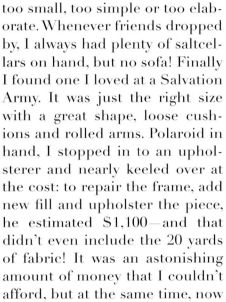

ACQUIRE *FLEA MARKETS*

Embrace the past for a glimpse into the future.

My rush starts early, well before I'm on the field or through the doors. My heart skips, my palms sweat, and I can feel myself entering a familiar, dizzying trance. To the back I go, weaving through the aisles, tempted at every turn to stop, but I don't—not until I'm there. Not until the end can I begin again. And when I do, my eyes awaken to the world around me. Every shape takes form. Every color comes to life. Possibilities surge like waves. In a place crowded with the past, I see only the future. Relics, finely wrought and left to rust, will inspire the design of new items sure to find their way into magazines, onto shelves and into our homes. Trends ebb and flow at flea markets sooner than anywhere else, giving us glimpses into the future of style. Brass is the metal du jour. Mid-century is the new modern. But as quickly as a craze takes hold, it fades from memory even faster. What will tomorrow bring? Go to a flea market to find out—and take cash.

The Elephant's Trunk Flea Market in New Milford, Connecticut, is one of my favorites. I scored these treasures on a single Sunday, paying $60 in all. After getting it nice and clean, the embroidered hand towel brings homespun charm to coffee in the country (page 180).

PLANNING THE DAY

- **DO YOUR HOMEWORK** If you're looking for something specific, research it online first—you'll be in a better position to bargain.

- **CHOOSE COMPANY** Like any trip, go with people who have a similar pace. If you're in it for the long haul, you don't want to hear *I'm ready to go. Are you?*

- **DRESS THE PART** Wear comfy shoes and layers you can peel off as the day warms up. If you want to make deals, leave labels and flashy jewelry at home.

- **GET CASH** Some dealers take checks and credit cards, but you'll get better deals with cash. I give myself a budget and take only that amount. (Flash forward to my mad dash to the ATM, followed by a week of ramen noodles on gorgeous china.) If you don't have enough, give the dealer a deposit and go get the rest.

- **ARRIVE WHEN YOU WANT** If flashlights and wake-up calls aren't your thing, the recognizable stuff everybody wants might be gone when you get there. But if you want smalls, go when you want. Dealers are also more likely to give better deals later in the day.

5 ⁰⁰ ea.

Center left: *After cleaning up the old pipe stand I bought for $5, I turned it into a breakfast server for passing toast, soft-boiled eggs and spoons (page 179).*

NAVIGATING A FLEA MARKET

- **SWIM UPSTREAM** Get your lay of the land first with an online map. Start at the back, where booths won't be as picked over, and work your way forward.

- **GO BIG FIRST** If it's furniture you want, focus on that first. Scan the aisles quickly and slow down to look more closely if something catches your eye. Can't commit? Jot down the booth number or mark it on a map. I even ask dealers for their cell numbers. Finding a specific booth again can be a nightmare at big flea markets.

- **LOOK HIGH, BUY LOW** Study the items at higher end booths—the ones merchandised like stores—then try to find them for less in junkier spots.

- **DIG IN** There's good stuff in all of those boxes other people pass up. It may need a little work, but you'll score.

- **PULL THE TRIGGER** If you don't, someone else will. Making a decision is hard sometimes, but when you find something you love at a fair price, buy it.

- **GET SOCIAL** Some dealers are walking encyclopedias. When you come across one who's knowledgeable, stay a while—that's how you learn.

- **PLAY NICE** Let's face it—you're at a flea market because you want a deal, but it's not going to happen if you insult a dealer by low-balling. If they're asking $100, don't counter with $20. Ask them what their lowest price would be—say it's $90—and if that still seems high, offer them $70 and go from there. Dealers worked hard to find their wares and are trying to make a living.

- **TAKE TWO** Make another round if you're up for it—you'll catch things you missed the first time. Circle back to booths with items that caught your eye early on; you might find a better deal.

The hand needle-pointed mid-century modern rug, bottom left, and box full of 1950s brass and rosewood Indonesian flatware, middle left, are two things I passed up at the end of the day because my budget was spent.

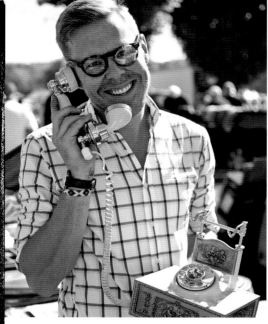

FAVORITE FLEA MARKET FINDS

Combing through flea markets is one of my favorite weekend activities no matter where I am, city or country. Here are a few of my entertaining go-tos that I reach for time and again.

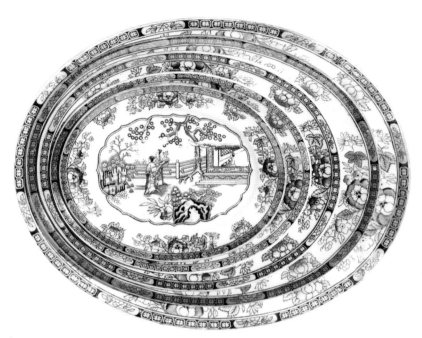

This chinoiserie set has served up hors d'oeuvres at many a party. A graduated set of five transferware platters, Chelsea Flea Market, New York City; $45.

This decorative opaline vase has held every type of flower from the garden; Scott Antique Market, Atlanta, GA; $18.

With candlelight, three are better than one or two; mahogany turned-wood candlestick, Brimfield Antique Show, Brimfield, MA; $15.

LOOK FOR METAL INSERTS AND CANDLESTICKS SEPARATELY. MIX AND MATCH MATERIALS TO GET A FRESH LOOK. I FOUND THE SILVER-PLATED INSERT AT THE ROSE BOWL FLEA MARKET IN PASADENA. ALSO LOOK FOR INSERTS FOR CAKE PEDESTALS AND COMPOTES.

The cheerful colors of this cloisonné compote complement any crudité combination; Metrolina Vintage & Antique Show, Charlotte, NC; $12.

ACQUIRE *THRIFT SHOPS*

Make it a habit of shopping thrift stores to score unique finds and support local causes.

Thrifting gives me the fix I need between flea markets. You never know what someone's going to donate, so I go as often as I can. Plus, it feels good to help a good cause. Thrift shops range from simple to elaborate, with prices and merchandise to match. On one end, you have the sweet ladies who volunteer their time, pricing everything for pennies to keep it moving. On the other, shrewd owners running consignment stores often know exactly what they have and price items accordingly. It all depends on the neighborhood and who's behind the register. My advice? Try every store once. If you don't find anything the first time but the prices are fair, go back. Thrifting is a way of life that fuels the modern mix, so dive in. Soon you'll need your fix, too.

Unlike at a flea market, where stuff is usually more spread out, things at a thrift store can pile up. After a while, items start to look alike. Keep your eyes focused, scanning shapes, colors, materials and finishes—everything you've discovered is here.

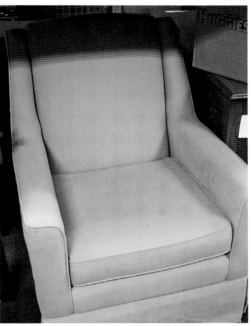

THRIFTING LIKE A PRO

- **LOCATE STORES** Find local Goodwill and other large stores through their websites. Search for smaller, charity-driven shops and read reviews at The Thrift Shopper online.

- **MOVE ON UP** Visit stores in nicer neighborhoods. Disposable income often generates disposable high-end merchandise.

- **LOOK FOR STRAYS** If you don't see a complete set of glasses or dishware, make sure you check the shelves above and below—strays have a way of wandering off.

- **FILL A BAG** Some shops let you fill a bag with merchandise for a fixed price. I've fit enough china in a grocery bag to have a dinner party for eight.

- **MAKE FRIENDS** Get to know the people who run the stores you frequent. Sometimes they'll give you a call when items come in that you might like.

- **SHOP SEASONALLY** People clean out their houses and make donations as the seasons change. Another prime time to shop is after the first of the year, when people make room for holiday purchases.

- **CHECK BACK OFTEN** You never know what someone's going to donate—or when. Find out the days new merchandise comes in. And don't be afraid to leave empty-handed; there's always a next time.

- **INSPECT UPHOLSTERY** Unless you plan to reupholster a piece immediately, there's a risk of bed bugs. Inspect upholstery thoroughly before you buy. Check every crack, crevice, seam and fold. A visual inspection isn't 100%, so if you don't want to run the risk, move on.

- **GIVE BACK** Donate your own unwanted things from time to time—it keeps the cycle going for everyone.

Top left: On 1stdibs, a set of these Fornasetti cocktail coasters goes for $1,200. But I paid $12 at a thrift shop for eight of them, which I use as appetizer plates. There's nothing lucky about it: if you educate your eyes and take time to look, the world opens up.

FAVORITE THRIFTING FINDS

When I'm out on the hunt looking for that IT score, I never know what is going to catch my eye. Our good friend Jessika calls these finds cheap and cheerful, and that's exactly what they are, but with a bit of chic thrown in. Here are a few of my fave finds from thrift shops.

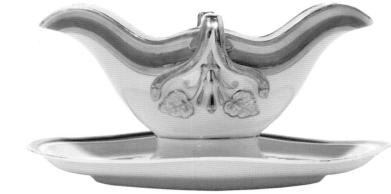

This saucy French porcelain gravy boat is perfect for holiday tables, but I use it for flower arrangements all year long. Goodwill, Des Moines, IA, $4.

The painterly purple fish scale pattern on this Czech coffee service sets the stage for dessert. Savers, Brookfield, CT $15.

LOOK FOR CONSIGNMENT AND SECONDHAND SHOPS IN UPSCALE AREAS. I FIND YOU SPEND A BIT MORE, BUT THE SELECTIONS CAN REALLY BE GOOD.

I swept this brass crumber right up off the shelf. It needed to be polished, but I saw past the tarnish. Salvation Army, Portchester, NY, $5.

A zebra may never change its stripes, but these glasses are not for juice anymore. Cocktails are served! Goodwill, Trenton, NJ, $2.

THRIFT THE FRIENDLY SKIES

Finding great stuff when you're on the road is the fun part; getting it home is another story. Here's how to do it on a budget:

- **CHECK IT** Shipping can be pricey. If you're flying home, sometimes it's cheaper to check a box with your finds than to mail it.

- **PULL A SWITCH** Ship back your clothes, then stuff non-fragile items into a suitcase. Even a rug will fit if the suitcase is large enough.

- **CARRY ON** That's how I usually bring home smalls. Give security a head's up if there's anything questionable in your bag. Lead crystal looks opaque on a scanner; large serving pieces can be iffy too. After a trip to Scott's, I once carried a pair of wrought iron andirons shaped like owls through the Atlanta airport. Remember, never try to carry on sharp objects.

- **GO GREYHOUND** It's not glamorous, but it gets the job done. Years back, I bought a one-way ticket for a brass and Lucite bar cart from Miami to New York—we both needed a stiff drink after that one.

ACQUIRE *TAG SALES*

In the disposable tangle of a stranger's trash, find treasure.

Although I plan every fork, flower and foil-wrapped confection on a table, when it comes to finding tag sales, I'm more spontaneous. This is how it usually goes: Sunday at 11-ish, I'm either coming or going from a flea market, depending on my life choices the night before. I'm rounding a corner when the flash of a neon sign sparks a thrill I crave. "Can we?" I ask Jaithan (letting him think that *no* is an option). Abruptly I turn; the trees are leafy and old, the houses grand—telltale signs of treasures ahead. I slow to a crawl, catch the glint of gold and stop. "Be right back," and in seconds I see an old carving set in pristine condition. "Maybe I'll cook tonight," I say to Jaithan in the car, tracing a thumb over handles gilded in gold. "Grilled chicken."

Every other summer, I'll have a tag sale of my own, clearing house of items I've loved and used so that others might do the same. Grouping objects of similar style, color or material creates instant collections, turning browsers into buyers.

STREET WIDE
TAG
SALES
9:00 AM - 4:00 PM

SCORING AT TAG SALES

- **STEER TOWARD OLDER** Stick to older, upscale neighborhoods, where people have been accumulating longer.

- **MAP A ROUTE** Check Craigslist and local papers to find sales. Two apps I like are Yard Sale Treasure Map and Garage Sale Tracker.

- **TAKE CASH** Include smaller bills to make it easier on everyone.

- **RESPECT OTHERS** The no-brainer stuff goes first, but don't arrive too much before the start time—it's just rude. And look out for lawns, dogs and kids. You're there to score a deal, not a lawsuit.

- **BE CHATTY** Talk to the seller about the pieces you're interested in; they might give you a better deal.

- **ASK NICELY** People don't always put out everything from the start. Ask if there might be anything else for sale.

- **CLEAN UP LATER** Find better deals later in the day, when sellers don't want to pack up.

Middle right: You'll have to dig harder at a tag sale than anyplace else. There are no volunteers organizing wares by color or dealers merchandising booths. But amid all those cassette tapes and power tools, you can find ultrachic treasures at next-to-nothing prices.

FAVORITE TAG SALE FINDS

Tag sales, to me, are the true meaning of "one man's trash is another man's treasure." They can be a hit or miss, depending on who is selling. They could be full of tools, toys or junk. I put many miles on our car driving from sale to sale, sometimes crossing three state lines in one day. Here are a few of my favorite finds.

Deviled eggs are the perfect accompaniment for this Picasso-esque Italian mid-century modern rooster plate. Geneva, IL, $5.

This brass swan magazine rack flew back east with me from a roadside sale. He is now sitting pretty, holding my favorite titles. Omaha, NE, $25.

I got along swimmingly with this blue milk glass dolphin candlestick that looks great with a Lucite and silver faux candle. Canaan, CT. $15.

LOOK FOR TABLEWARE AND OBJECTS WITH DOLPHIN MOTIFS. REMINISCENT OF SOFAS, TABLES AND MIRRORS MADE IN THE EARLY 1800S, THEY ADD A CHIC AQUATIC SPLASH TO ANY ROOM.

Adam and Eve might have broken a tooth trying the take a bite out of this turquoise marble apple that I picked out of a box. It now lives with others in a brass bowl. Highpoint, NC, $1.

Vintage seahorses embellish these tall tumblers, just waiting to serve sea breezes. Atlanta, GA, each 50c.

Truffle mushrooms might be considered culinary gold, but these beauties were foraged right from a grimy garage bay. Tampa, FL, $2.

LOOK FOR ACCESSORIES OR TABLEWARE WITH WHIMSY. THEY CAN TAKE A TABLEAU FROM TRADITIONAL TO TRUE-TO-YOU.

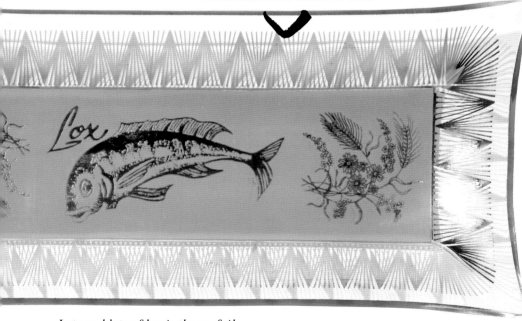

Lots and lots of lox is the no-fail brunch sidekick. But this cute dish makes a quirkier statement on my desk. Bridgeport, CT, $1.

ACQUIRE ONLINE

Think of the Internet as another way to supplement your search for cool finds.

- **EBAY** If you know the manufacturer and pattern name of any china, glassware or cutlery you're looking for to complete a set, you can probably find it here. I usually don't have the patience for auctions, so the *Buy Now* feature is a must.

- **CRAIGSLIST** You can score incredible things all over the country for reasonable prices. Enter specific key words (brass chandelier, for instance) to get the best results.

- **SHOPGOODWILL.COM** Goodwill Stores from across the country often save their best wares for online auctions. There's no *Buy Now* option, so you have to bid. Check back frequently for new listings.

- **ONE KING'S LANE** Get your daily dose of designer style delivered to your in-box. Check out the vintage section for great tableware, art and objects at price points well below retail. It's one of the best-curated, most beautiful online shopping experiences.

- **ETSY** Find gorgeous handmade things from around the world—pottery and woodenware are two of my favorites. Make sure you're searching the right section when you key in a term.

- **REPLACEMENTS, LTD.** Here's another fantastic resource for filling in sets of china, silver and crystal. Even if you don't know the pattern, they'll work with you to figure it out.

- **INSTAGRAM SHOPS** Socially savvy retailers are creating shops on Instagram. You might have to click around a bit to buy; if that doesn't work, message the owner directly.

ACQUIRE *ESTATE SALES*

Reimagine old things to tell your story in the circle of life.

Not all estate sales happen at estates, by any stretch. I've been to many a *chateau nouveau*—big houses with big mortgages and empty rec rooms that cost a fortune to build and even more to furnish. (Hence, the *For Sale* sign out front.) Some sales, though, are truly grand—sad, yes, a little creepy at times, but grand. If the owners lived in the house for a while, you can find furniture, tableware, linens, books and memorabilia that tell a captivating story of their tastes and travels going back decades. Those are the sales where I take my time, sifting through every box, buffet and built-in for hidden gems. I'm respectful but focused; the owners want to sell and I'm there to buy. And after all of my finds are cleaned and washed, I'll tell a new story in the circle of life.

I struck gold in this 1920s brick house in an older neighborhood. I searched every room, from the basement to the attic— even the garage!

SHOPPING ESTATE SALES

- **FIND LOCAL SALES** Start your search at EstateSales.net, where you can often find pictures of items for sale or a floor plan of the house. Check Craigslist, local newspapers and yard sale apps.

- **SHOP ESTABLISHED AREAS** Estate sales are usually better in older neighborhoods. Look for stately houses in urban and rural areas that are more established.

- **GO EARLY AND LATE** Arrive early on the first day and the last. As with flea markets and tag sales, you'll have more to choose from early but might find better deals later.

- **MIND YOUR MANNERS** Most estate sales happen when a homeowner decides to downsize or someone has passed on. Yes, they can be creepy, but if a reputable company is in charge and the prices are fair, you can easily overlook that. Be respectful in case a homeowner or relative is present.

- **SIGN UP FOR EMAILS** If it's an option, add your name to a mailing list to find out first about upcoming sales.

Bottom left: *Inspect linens for holes and tableware for chips and cracks that might bother you. This damask tablecloth had seen better days, but the monogram on it could have been easily turned into a stylish pillow.*

FAVORITE ESTATE SALE FINDS

I have a different connection to the pieces I buy from an estate sale, having seen firsthand where art hung or where a vase sat on a fireplace mantel. These were all items that were collected and loved, heirlooms that are now going to be part of my life.

This little pup is English Staffordshire embellished with pink luster. He was perched on a stack of art books when I found him. Elm Grove, WI, $27.

These faux malachite candlesticks were standing strong on a modern sideboard holding plain white candles. Now hot pink beeswax will spark a flame. Rancho Mirage, CA, $15.

LOOK FOR SMALL OBJECTS ON TABLES FIRST, THEN OPEN DRAWERS AND DOORS ON FURNITURE TO FIND OTHER ITEMS. DON'T FORGET TO LOOK IN THE ATTIC, BASEMENT, BACKYARD AND GARAGE, IF ALLOWED. ASK ABOUT RUGS, CURTAINS, WINDOW HARDWARE AND EVEN FIXED LIGHTING FIXTURES, LIKE SCONCES AND CHANDELIERS.

Gilded fruit and swags decorate this Meissen plate plucked from a Sheraton hutch. Farm stand fruit never tasted so sweet. Kansas City, MO, $25.

THE ESSENTIAL *ACQUIRE* KIT

Don't waste time when you're on a mission.
Pack the essentials that will keep you going all
day long.

- Design Notebook—Keep dimensions, ideas
  and inspirational photos in one place;
  include paint chips and fabric swatches
- Tape measure
- Magnifying glass
- Hand sanitizer
- Bug spray
- Lip balm
- Sunscreen
- Band-Aids
- Hand wipes
- Poncho
- Umbrella
- Hat
- Snacks
- Water
- Flashlight

When you pack your kit,
throw in a couple of extra
bags and make sure they're
sturdy. Most of the ones you'll
get when you're on the hunt are
the flimsy plastic kind. Buy a set
of plates or glasses and they'll break
before you even get back to the car!

I'm always finding fancy dinner napkins at thrift shops on Manhattan's Upper East Side. Once home, I'll soak them in water and The Laundress all-purpose bleach alternative to spot treat any stains and finish them off on a gentle cycle in the washer.

I'm always trying to wrangle one person or another into going to a Goodwill. In culinary school, my friend Jenny indulged me and even grew to like it herself. But back in high school, Abby was a different story. She loved tabletop as much as I did. Every time we pulled into the parking lot, we'd practically trample over each other and everyone inside trying to get to the bric-a-brac aisle first.

One day I found a set of Bombay Red transferware ironstone made in England by John Maddock & Sons. It was nearly a full service for eight with several serving pieces—all for less than $20. Some of them were discolored in spots, but I didn't care. There must be some way to get them clean—I just needed to figure out how. Quickly I gathered up the set, piling into my arms as much as I could to take to the register. I was on my way back for the rest when Abby came barreling up, waving a single saucer.

"Look what I found!" she said.

"Look what *I* found!" I countered, pointing to the pile of transferware.

After a friendly brawl over china (not our last), Abby conceded, though to this day we'll often lend each other sets of china, including this one, whenever we need them. Eagerly I packed up the pieces and headed home to begin the formidable task of bringing them back to life.

While my younger brothers played football on the lawn, I soaked a set of china in a warm water bath and Efferdent. Somewhere I'd read that those fizzy, fast-acting enzymes could clean more than just dentures, and to my astonishment, they worked! Suddenly I realized that all of that gorgeous stuff I'd seen catering parties at houses on Saturdays and in tarnished piles at the flea market on Sundays—extraordinary, quality items that, for one reason or another, had gone unloved and left for garbage—might possibly, in my hands, become beautiful again.

Some years later, I realized that as much as I soak, scour and scrub a piece trying to restore it, sometimes my hands just aren't enough. I was looking for a chandelier to hang in my third apartment and decided to go to Braswell Galleries in Norwalk, one of my favorite places

INSTAGRAM MOMENT: EVEN AFTER SO MANY YEARS, THE RED BOMBAY TRANSFERWARE PLATES ARE STILL MY GO-TO PATTERN FOR A MODERN MIX PLACE SETTING.

at the time for estate merchandise at fair prices. I passed up one after another hanging in glittering clusters with expensive price tags until there, in a pile of twisted glass, I spotted one that looked as though it had been ripped right out of the ceiling. Copper wires were encrusted with plaster; glass bobeches looked brown with nicotine soot. Even though it was in bits and pieces, I knew it was great, like one of those pretty chandeliers that I'd seen at antique shows for hundreds. I paid $50 for it, raced home, rolled up my sleeves and went to work.

Meticulously I took the fixture apart, soaking every piece in a degreaser to break up the grime. Those parts that couldn't be removed for soaking I cleaned with a toothbrush and Q-tips until every piece came clean. To electrify it, I turned to the services of an expert. I began my search in Greenwich, where one craftsman quoted me $60 an arm. Then I searched in the next town, Port Chester, where I found someone willing to do the job for half that amount. Restoration, I learned, is no different from any other service: it always pays to shop around.

From the Accessory Store in Stamford, I picked up eight black shades together with new candlestick covers. A couple of months later, I was browsing an estate sale in New Canaan and found a box of cut crystal pendants far better than the ones on my fixture, most of which had gone missing. Thanks to the help of a skilled craftsman trained in the art of restoration, along with a mix of new and old accessories, the chandelier I'd found in pieces now hung splendidly in my apartment. Every ounce of elbow grease I'd put into it, every dollar I'd spent helped transform a neglected relic of the past into a thing of beauty.

Now that you've discovered what to look for and where, in this chapter you'll learn how to restore your finds using my favorite products, tools and techniques. Sometimes it's as easy as what I call the "instant gratification approach" to treasure hunting: find a diamond in the rough, give it a good wash or polish, use it right away. Other times, you'll want to call upon the services of an expert. More often than not, restoration takes effort, but when a hidden gem finally reveals itself, or a family heirloom takes on glorious new life, the end results always shine.

RESTORE *GLASS*

Repair chipped or cloudy glass by calling in a pro

You're always going to find vintage glassware in different conditions. Sometimes at flea markets, I pour a little water into a piece just to see if the dirt will come out when I wash it. A few water marks on an inexpensive vase with a great shape that you're going to use for flowers don't matter—no one will ever notice them. Once you're home, restoring glass can be as easy as running a set of found goblets through the dishwasher and enjoying a bottle of wine in them that night. But accidents do happen—one minute you're making a toast or doing dishes and the next you're left with a chip (or more) on a glass, so you put it right into the garbage. C'est la vie, right? Well, not always. You might be surprised what skilled artisans can do to mend broken glass—and hearts.

CLOUDED Calcium buildup from hard water clouds the insides of these fine crystal decanters that I bought at a junk shop.

CHIPPED Original stoppers for decanters are often hard to come by, so this one has small chips in need of repair.

CRYSTAL CLEAR

High-end antique stores are treasure troves of inspiration. In James Robinson on Park Avenue, I saw a magnificent crystal decanter, a fine antique priced at over $1,000. Months later, at a junk shop I saw two decanters in a similar style, *opposite*, their insides thickly clouded with calcium deposits etched into the glass from years of hard water. For $5 apiece, I bought them anyway, then sent them to Dean Schulefand of China and Crystal Repair, who polished out the insides, ground down tiny chips and restored the decanters to a brilliant shine—all for less than $150 each. Now I have a fine one-of-a-kind pair.

SMOOTH FINISH

Glass is fragile and sometimes it chips. Take this handblown compote with an R monogram; it's one of my favorites. I use it for everything from grilled shrimp at cocktail hour to grapes on a cheese platter. When I nicked it clearing dishes after a party, I thought for sure that was it. But after picking myself up off the floor, I collected the pieces and called Dean again, who ground down the entire rim and polished it to a smooth finish. It's a tiny bit shorter now, but still as gorgeous (and usable) as ever.

THIS MONOGRAMMED CRYSTAL COMPOTE IS ONE OF MY FAVORITES. WHEN I CHIPPED IT CLEANING UP AFTER A PARTY, INSTEAD OF TOSSING IT OUT, I CALLED ON A PRO, WHO WORKED MAGIC TO BRING IT BACK TO LIFE.

YOU CAN USUALLY CLEAN UP glassware that isn't clouded yourself. Call it criminal, but I almost always run my finds through the gentle cycle on the dishwasher at least once for a good clean. Reality check: I'm about to set a table for dinner with mid-century goblets from the Goodwill, not make an appearance on *Antiques Roadshow*. But if you're a purist, wash everything by hand with lukewarm water and mild dishwashing soap. Keep a set of good brushes on hand, like the ones on page 104—the long, skinny tips are must-haves for decanters. To dry them, insert a rolled-up piece of paper towel. Stick them in the sun to speed things up—you have cocktails to make!

PUNCH LINE

Punch bowls aren't just for punch. As you'll see, they're one of those versatile essentials that add drama anywhere they go. I bought this pressed glass one with a pedestal years ago and have used it in every place I've lived until a friend who was helping me move chipped part of the rim. Judging by my hysteria, he probably thought it was my great-great-*great*-grandmother's, who used it for serving wassail to the Queen of England. We all have things that are sentimental to us; they might not be valuable but they're special—and worth restoring. Dean Schulefand of China & Crystal Repair worked his magic again, adding glass where it was missing (you can barely tell!) and polishing it to perfection. Find an artisan near you who can work miracles on chipped, cracked or cloudy glassware. Or drop Dean a line—he's repaired glass (and china) from Hawaii to Maine.

RESTORE *UTENSILS*

Fix broken flatware and serving pieces so they look like new.

Most of the utensils you'll find on the hunt can easily be revived with a quick wash and polish. But sometimes, you'll come across damaged pieces at next-to-nothing prices that make it worth calling in a pro. Skilled artisans can just as easily give broken heirloom utensils brilliant new life.

Here's a chic way to serve baked dishes and gratins. It's an English spade with a bone handle that I found on a table bound for scrap.

Since I scored a deal on these mother-of-pearl utensils with sterling silver ferrules—forks, a table knife and a cake server—I decided to go the extra step and have them professionally restored.

SPARKLE & SHINE

When I go digging in boxes of tarnished silver at a flea market, I don't have a clue what I'm looking for. But one thing's for sure—I'll know it when I find it. I loved the bone handle of the spade, *opposite,* but it was missing an end piece and the silver plate had worn through. Mother-of-pearl flatware adds jewelry to tables; these looked more like Jaws just had lunch. Antique utensils in special materials like these bring character to tables and buffets,

and thanks to the help of a skilled metalsmith, mine have never looked better. David Friedman of Friedman Silversmiths replated the spade, cleaned and polished the handle, then added a new ball finial. To restore the mother-of-pearl pieces, he detached their handles, glued back the broken pieces and replated the blades; then he buffed, polished and reset them. Now I have an array of unusual utensils that will bring vintage charm to any modern mix.

LOOK PAST THE TARNISH, DIRT, AND WHATEVER ELSE. YOU CAN FIND INTERESTING SERVING PIECES, FROM ENGLISH FISH SETS WITH PIERCED DETAILING BUT WORN SILVER, TO MONOGRAMMED SILVER ICE TONGS WITH FALCON-CLAW TINES THAT LOOK LIKE THEY MIGHT HAVE BEEN RUN OVER BY A TRUCK. MOST LIKELY THEY CAN BE RESTORED. IT'S DEFINITELY WORTH THE EFFORT AND MAKES GREAT DINNER CONVERSATION.

RESTORE *METAL*

Revive old metal objects yourself or enlist the help of an expert.

I always loved a good Pepsi Challenge ad—all those everyday people, just like you and me, preferring— shockingly—the taste of Pepsi over the leader, Coca- Cola. I'd love to do that kind of blind test at a flea market. John, here, just paid through the roof for a Gorham silver stuffing spoon polished to perfection. Sally, on the other hand, got a deal: she bought the same spoon, heavily tarnished, for half the price. And there you have it, America: put a little extra time or money into a metal treasure you score for a song, and you'll make the switch, too.

For your electric drill, pick up a kit with cotton buffing wheels for polishing copper and brass to a high shine.

SIZING UP COPPER

Back in middle school, while most of the other kids were playing kickball, my grandparents and I watched Julia Child make fancy French food in a kitchen filled with cooper. But you don't have to be dishing up coq au vin to appreciate the metal's superior conductivity for cooking or the warmth it adds to a kitchen. New copper cookware can be expensive, so I'm always on the lookout for sturdy secondhand pots. I bought the two above for $60 at a flea market. One of them even had its original cover with a poured-iron handle. Sometimes all they need is a good cleaning, but when there's pitting on the inside of a pot or the copper is showing through the lining, you must have the piece retinned by a professional.

I SPOTTED THIS JUMBO COPPER POT ON A SOGGY DAY AT BRIMFIELD, BUT THERE JUST WASN'T ANY MORE ROOM IN MY CART! IT WOULD HAVE BEEN A STEAL AT $90, EVEN THOUGH THE LINING WOULD HAVE HAD TO BE RETINNED.

HIGH SHINE

Reviving copper cookware, like any other professional restoration, is an investment. Retinning copper is one of those ancient art forms as elemental as sharpening knives. The best coppersmiths, such as Jim Hamann of East Coast Tinning, have sure hands and an eye for subtlety to achieve uniform results. After retinning the lining of my pots so they're food-safe, Jim buffed and polished the exterior to a high shine. Once your pieces are looking new, take care to protect them. Never scorch or scour tinned pots and pans. Soak them overnight in warm water and dish-washing liquid to soften and remove residue. Sprinkle with Bar Keepers Friend inside and out, scrub with a non-abrasive brush and wash as normal. Dry them off completely, then use Peek Metal Polish and a soft cloth to restore their gleam.

CREATE AN INSTANT HEIRLOOM
WITH PERSONAL STYLE BY HAVING
A PIECE STAMPED. I ASKED JIM THE
COPPERSMITH TO STAMP ONE OF MY
POTS WITH P.H.F. FOR PINE HILL FARM
AND THE YEAR IT WAS RESTORED.

LOOK FOR VINTAGE COPPER POTS, RESTORE THEM TO A HIGH SHINE AND GIVE THEM AWAY AS WEDDING GIFTS. CULINARY TYPES IN PARTICULAR WILL APPRECIATE THEIR WARM LUSTER WITH INSIDES AS BRIGHT AS NEW DIMES. PERSONALIZE THEM WITH A COUPLE'S MONOGRAM AND THE YEAR THEY WERE MARRIED.

PAST THEIR PRIME

Ever come across something metal that brings back a long-forgotten memory? Something that takes you back in time but looks way past its prime? Dottie used these old potato graters to make pierogi; the smallest oil can once serviced her Singer sewing machine; and I found the Moscow mule set at a flea market. They're not valuable objects, but they're special to me. Just as a coat of paint can revive a drab room or freshen up old furniture, metal refinishing can dramatically extend the life of an object or alter its use entirely. To restore these faded treasures to their former glory, once again I called in the pros.

TREASURED AGAIN

A trio of American metalsmith companies worked their magic, *opposite*. I had Victoria Plating Company refinish the potato graters in brass to use as passing trays with an industrial glam vibe. Inspired by a sterling silver vermouth dispenser I once spotted in a vintage magazine, I had David Friedman of Friedman Silversmiths plate Dottie's version in silver. It takes pride of place on our bar beside two other sentimental favorite oil cans salvaged from my grandfather's garage. Jim Hamann of East Coast Tinning cleaned and polished the copper on one can, and Victoria Plating finished the other in brass. I wouldn't store vermouth in them, but I will fill them up for a party. Since guests would be drinking from the Moscow mule mugs bought for a steal, I had Jim go the extra step to retin and polish them. Turn to page 209 to see their debut at a Derby party in the country.

THE POWER OF POLISH

Never underestimate the power of a little polish—and a lot of elbow grease—to revive tarnished metal. This pierced globe was a lighting fixture. I polished it in five easy steps:

STEP ONE: Wash using a soft sponge with warm water and mild soap. **STEP TWO:** Remove heavy stains with Bar Keepers Friend. **STEP THREE:** Rinse with warm water. **STEP FOUR:** Dry with a soft cotton cloth. **STEP FIVE:** Polish with Peek.

If a favorite piece of china or pottery breaks into clean pieces, don't lose hope. With a clear-drying glue or epoxy, you can often make repairs to damaged ceramics, like this pie server and luncheon plate, that are nearly invisible. Follow the directions on your adhesive carefully, then use the technique, opposite, to allow them to set.

RESTORE *CERAMICS*

Bring beauty back to broken or stained ceramics yourself.

I have an owl's ears for breakage. I could be styling a shoot, hear the slightest clink clear across a house and think the absolute worst. Despite even the best intentions, things happen to our treasures. Like glass, ceramic pieces can easily break, and if they're special to us in some way, hearts break right along with them. Discoloration is also often inevitable over time, leaving ironstone, in particular, with unsightly brown stains. Of course, every case will be different. Some repairs, like the two I describe here, are those you can easily do yourself, but for pieces with more extensive damage, you're better off contacting a professional. I've used Ark Restoration & Design in New York.

PLOP, PLOP, FIZZ, FIZZ

One of my favorite household "hacks" is using Efferdent—yes, the stuff your grandparents used for cleaning their dentures—to remove stains from ironstone. Solutions like bleach are way too harsh—and possibly harmful—but Efferdent is gentle and effective enough to get the job done. All you need is water, a container large enough to hold the pieces you plan to soak, a couple Efferdent tablets and a little bit of patience. Here's how:

• **FILL** your container to the brim with water and drop in 3 or 4 tablets (depending on how many pieces you are soaking and how big they are). The water will turn blue.

• **WAIT** to remove your pieces (or even check on them) until the water has turned completely clear. Give the tablets a chance to do their work. I usually allow a full 24 hours to be sure the water is crystal clear before pulling my pieces out.

• **WASH** with normal soap and water. If the stain is lightened but not completely gone, you may want to repeat the process.

SECOND ACT Gluing broken ceramics back together is only half the battle. Unless they set properly, they are bound to break again. Enter what I like to call the "salt solution." Fill a large, deep dish with run-of-the-mill table salt. After gluing, hold the piece in place for a short time to adhere, then position the unbroken portion in the salt to hold it steady. Wait several hours before removing it so that the epoxy has plenty of time to dry. This will give your piece its very best chance at a second act.

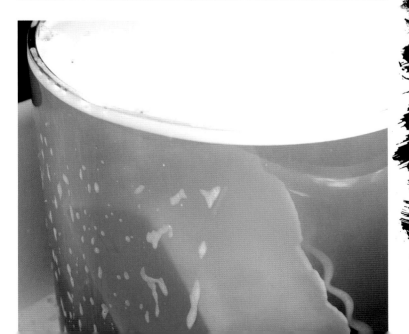

RESTORE *TEXTILES*

Give fresh new life to vintage sheets, tablecloths and napkins.

Secondhand sheets and napkins can give us the skeeves, and it's easy to understand why: they've been used in ways that are simply, shall we say, closer to home. But if you think about it, the sheets at hotels and the napkins at restaurants have seen a lot more use than anything you'll find at a flea market. So don't get creeped out the next time you're at a tag sale and see a set of cocktail napkins or pillowcases in a print you love. Even antique white linens that have yellowed over time can be brought back to life.

LAUNDRY DAY

You'll often find vintage sheets, napkins, towels and tablecloths in pristine piles at flea markets. Dig through the crumpled heaps beside them for better deals—and don't be deterred by stains. Acids in the air can discolor cotton and linen fibers, turning even the brightest whites an unsightly yellow with time. But you can bring vintage linens back to life with a few simple steps. The pros might not agree, but these are my real-life techniques that will freshen up most of your finds.

- **INSPECT** linens carefully for any holes, tears or broken threads before you buy. Hot climates are especially damaging, turning fibers dry and brittle.

- **SOAK** linens overnight in non-chlorine detergent. Avoid bleach, as it can damage the fibers. Do not wring clean wet linens; instead, roll them in a towel to remove excess water.

- **WASH** most linens on a gentle cycle with detergent. For lace and pulled work, launder by hand.

- **DRY** linens on a folding rack or flat on a towel, never in the dryer.

- **IRON** like a pro. Invest in a Rowenta iron and a Brabantia ironing board. These will make the job so much easier.

- **STORE** freshly laundered linens in a cool, dry place without natural light, as it can fade them over time.

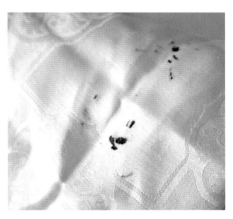

IN A SPOT If a tablecloth or napkins get stained and you don't have time to wash them right away, wet them thoroughly, roll them in a towel to remove excess water and place them in a plastic bag in the freezer. Keeping the stain wet helps prevent it from setting in.

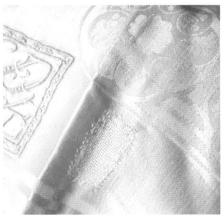

AS GOOD AS NEW Don't let a repair stop you from buying vintage textiles—if it's a good one. This napkin was part of a monogrammed set of 12 I bought at a tag sale. Years back, when one of them tore, the owner had it repaired to perfection by an expert.

RESTORE *WOOD*

Revitalize the character of wood furniture and objects.

Natural wood infuses a home with soul. In our kitchen at Pine Hill, I keep my collection of antique wooden spoons, bowls and breadboards proudly on display and within arm's reach. Remember, never leave wooden pieces soaking in the sink; that's when the wood cracks. After use, wash and dry quickly. Over time, wood pieces can lose their finish, just as furniture can. Here are a few tips, tricks and products you can use to breathe life back into natural wood. Try them first before you call in a pro.

BEFORE When wood serveware (cutting boards, bowls and utensils) starts to look dry and light, revitalize it with mineral oil and a beeswax conditioner.

AFTER Re-oiling dry wood brings back the grain's natural depth. Conditioning wood serveware helps protect it from food and moisture.

DO-IT-YOURSELF

Natural wood furniture can get beat up over time, but keep in mind it's not all made alike. Different woods and qualities benefit from different quick-fix solutions. Here are some you might want to consider before deciding to take it to a pro.

- Clean with a fine steel wool and Murphy Oil Soap.
- To remove a water ring, try mayonnaise.
- For covering scratches or filling small ones, some options are scratch polish, wood filler crayons, coffee grinds or tea bags, eyebrow pencil, marking pens, shoe polish.
- To fill a deeper scratch, rub in the meat of a walnut then polish with a soft cloth.
- If all else fails, paint presents a whole range of options.

TIME TO CALL IN A PRO. WHEN I WAS LOOKING FOR A DINING TABLE TO USE AT PINE HILL, I COULDN'T PASS UP THIS ONE THAT I FOUND ON CRAIGSLIST FOR $100. IT'S A QUALITY PIECE MADE BY DREXEL HERITAGE, SO I CALLED MY FRIEND BRIAN TRUDEAU, WHO PATCHED THE VENEER, STRIPPED, SANDED, STAINED AND REFINISHED THE PIECE TO PERFECTION.

RESTORE *TOOLS OF THE TRADE*

Build an arsenal of tools and products to restore your treasures and keep them looking like new.

You might not be able to repair King Tut's beard, but you can easily bring beauty back to secondhand treasures neglected over time. This before all else: buy the right tools for the job. I learned that one at my Aunt Frannie's place, where every Saturday growing up we'd spend the day together doing housework. For each task, there was only one product we could use: baking soda helped get the laundry clean, Twinkle shined the copper and Pledge worked magic on wood. It was noble work for Aunt Fran, and I loved it just as much. Learn the right products, tools and techniques for a job, and revitalizing old things gets a whole lot easier.

PEEK METAL POLISH *Pure magic! I use it to bring high shine to all my copper, silver and brass. It's pricey (even on Amazon) but worth it.*

SPONGES & STEEL WOOL *Pick up a few Pop-Up sponges from Williams-Sonoma. Use non-abrasive scouring pads to clean the insides of copper pots, since they won't damage the tin lining. Fine steel wool gets the age off of glass bakeware and removes dark spots from copper and brass.*

WRIGHT'S SILVER CREAM *I like this product for polishing lightly tarnished silver. Bonus points for coming with its own sponge.*

STICK TO WHITE PAPER TOWELS AND LEAVE THE FUN PATTERNS FOR OTHER THINGS.

LOOK TO THE PAST FOR QUICK-CLEANING TECHNIQUES THAT HAVE STOOD THE TEST OF TIME. IN A PINCH, POLISH SILVER WITH TOOTHPASTE. DITTO FOR LEMON AND SALT ON COPPER AND BRASS. COMMERCIAL PRODUCTS KEEP THINGS IN TIP-TOP SHAPE, BUT SOMETIMES A HOME REMEDY WILL WORK JUST FINE.

BRASSO METAL POLISH *This is my first plan of attack on tarnished brass and Dirilyte. If a tray is heavily spotted, I'll use Brasso with fine steel wool and finish it off with Peek.*

BRUSHES *The German bottle brushes from Sur La Table are a must. They come in all different shapes for cleaning decanters and fine glassware.*

BOOS BLOCK *Two of John Boos Butcher Block products work wonders on wood cutting boards and bowls. The Mystery Oil is like a thin shampoo that revitalizes wood, while the Board Cream is more of a conditioner, forming a protective layer against moisture.*

OXICLEAN STAIN REMOVER *This one's a serious workhorse, good for cleaning colored linens and tablecloths. It also removes the shellac from marble, copper and brass objects with a good soak.*

BAR KEEPERS FRIEND *They're not lying about that either— we're BFFs in the kitchen! I use it to clean my cookware and the outside of my copper pots. But do your hands a favor: wear gloves.*

LEATHER LOTION *A good product for cleaning and replenishing leather trays, boxes, coasters and vintage suitcases. I've even used it on an old ottoman from the flea market that just needed a little lift.*

WEIMAN WAX AWAY *Dissolve candle wax from tablecloths without a lot of scraping. Drizzle the solvent on the wax, remove it with a clean, soft towel and launder as normal.*

DON'T LET A LITTLE HOUSEWORK MUCK UP YOUR NEW MANI. BUY A BIG BOX OF DISPOSABLE NITRILE GLOVES FROM LOWE'S AND STASH THEM UNDER THE SINK.

PFALTZGRAFF STONEWARE CLEANER *Remove stains (including metal marks left by flatware) from porcelain, ironstone and other ceramic materials.*

IT DOES THE WASHING SO YOU DON'T HAVE TO ...

I'm always looking for new ways of living with old things—and that includes getting them clean. When it comes to china, flatware and glass, nothing does the job better than a hot dishwasher. Use a non-abrasive detergent on a gentle cycle if you want. Of course, I won't put any knives, brass, gold plate, Dirilyte or flatware with special handles like mother-of-pearl in a dishwasher, but everything else is fair game. After all, I'm not spending a ton of money on this stuff, so I'm willing to take a few risks to save a lot of time and effort.

In the kitchen at Pine Hill Farm I display my curated collection of copper pots and pans on an antique wrought iron pot rack. I started collecting copper cookware while I was in culinary school. I love how it looks, but most of all how it cooks.

Before we all started to "curate" our playlists and Pinterest boards, our shelfies and shopping carts, we might have simply "edited" them. Since I work as an editor every day, scouting houses, styling photo shoots and sourcing products for stories, I'm always on the lookout for interesting or unusual things that can add personality to the pictures I produce. You can imagine how quickly things could start piling up if I didn't keep my shopping in check! Although nowadays I do edit my impulses to create a home that's just cluttered enough to make me happy, it wasn't always the case.

By the time I finished decorating my third apartment, I thought I'd finally hit my stride when it came to style. As a caterer with a budding addiction to flea markets, I had already amassed enough serveware of my own to throw a buffet dinner for a hundred. It was a collection more akin to a butler's pantry on Park Avenue than to an apartment in Connecticut. There were ironstone platters in every shape and size, hand-painted dishes from Limoges and depression glass everything. Silverware flaunted scrolls, flowers, monograms and coats of arms. Compotes and cake pedestals were stacked on bookcases to the ceiling; punch bowls sat one inside the other on a sideboard. Glassware and decanters in a mishmash of colors crowded a console, while candlesticks occupied every square inch on the mantel. For years I'd been buying things at flea markets and thrift shops simply because they had a good name or a good marking, not because I actually liked them. The end result looked more like a tag sale than a home!

Then I moved again, this time to a guest cottage in New Canaan, in which I finally decided to take the opportunity to edit my belongings—indeed, to curate them—whittling down the excess to the essentials I used and loved the most. After committing to an all-neutral palette so that everything I did keep would easily work together, I painted all of the walls a pretty stone color

INSTAGRAM MOMENT: AFTER A FUN DINNER WITH FRIENDS, I SNAPPED THIS PICTURE OF THE POST-PARTY BLUES RIGHT OUT OF THE DRYING RACK—TRANSFERWARE PLATTERS, HAND-PAINTED PLATES AND SILVER-PLATED SERVING PIECES.

and edited down my furniture to the pieces I'd painted white, accented with others in natural wood. Then I used that same rigorous point of view to curate my collections of serveware and accessories in silver, wood, cream and white china, clear glass and linen. In the pharmaceutical cabinet my grandfather had restored, I kept a versatile assortment of compotes, cake pedestals, trays, pitchers and platters. In a reproduction Sheridan sideboard with a veneer finish, I stored a handful of serving pieces and table accessories that I used time and again for the way I entertained, then sold the rest at a tag sale. On bookcases and occasional tables, I kept curated collections of vases, bowls and boxes, punctuated by off-kilter curiosities that added whimsy. After editing out everything that either I didn't love or that didn't work together, only the essential pieces remained. It was a liberating experience that would form the foundation for the layered mix I'd soon embrace.

In this chapter, you too will learn to look with fresh eyes at your belongings as you begin to curate your own personal library of serveware and accessories. If you're just starting off, think of these as the building blocks—the basic types of pieces, both new and old, that you ought to look for first as you curate your arsenal of essentials. Now that you've discovered various materials and finishes to look for, where to find them and how to restore them, you can apply that knowledge to the kinds of multi-purpose objects you'll learn about here. If you can't yet commit to pieces in specific colors and patterns, stick to neutrals—they'll always serve you well. Then, once you become more comfortable with a look that suits your style, can you can start to layer in other essentials with more personality.

If you're anything like I am, very soon you'll find your curated basics growing into full-blown collections. I don't mean the traditional kind with a single type of object, material or pattern displayed en masse, but rather a more thoughtful and diversified assortment of decorative objects and serving pieces you actually live with every day and use to entertain well. Those are the types of real-life collections you curate over time, and they begin here.

CURATE *THE ESSENTIALS*

Build a library of key serving pieces and accessories.

After years of styling and hosting parties, I've identified a handful of key pieces every home should have. Call them the essentials—your go-to serveware and table accessories that will help you create unforgettable experiences with confidence. But that doesn't mean you have to dispose of everything you already own and start over. I'm simply giving you the tools to help you edit your belongings in favor of events that are more thoughtful but no less expressive of who you are as a host. Of all the parties we give and attend, aren't those often the best?

LOOK FOR GLASS COMPOTES IN GRADUATED SIZES TO CREATE YOUR OWN SET. UP YOUR GAME ON A CHIP AND DIP PLATTER OR USE THEM FOR SERVING JUMBO COCKTAILS, LIKE PINEAPPLE RUM PUNCH.

COMPOTES

Add slender good looks to buffets and tables with compotes in assorted sizes. Larger types are better for cold salads and side dishes, smaller for sauces and dips. For a sweet-treat centerpiece, fill a single compote with candy, or stack them up high to thrilling effect. Deploy a simple flower frog, and your blooms will defy the laws of gravity.

PUNCH BOWLS are the grand pooh-bahs of buffets.

PUNCH BOWLS

A punch bowl is the indispensable vessel for adding wow to a party, and there's nothing old-fashioned about it. When you're not serving punch, use it for dishing up cold salads and soups on a buffet or for icing down wine and champagne on a bar. For a quick and easy centerpiece, pot a punch bowl with orchids or ferns, then swap it out for mercury glass ornaments at the holidays.

LOOK FOR PEDESTALS AND PUNCH BOWLS BOTH SEPARATELY AND TOGETHER. IF YOU FIND ONE OR THE OTHER YOU LIKE, BUY IT—YOU'LL EVENTUALLY FIND A PARTNER THAT FITS.

TUREENS & COVERED DISHES

Put a soup, stew or simple side dish in a tureen and let the oohs and aahs begin. Ditch the lid and make a potpie, or fill it with flowers in single varieties. Display tureens and covered dishes in different sizes on a sideboard when you're not using them. Pair antiques like these with colorful, clean-lined platters for a modern mix.

SERVING PIECES

Keep an eye out for essential serving pieces, both vintage and new. Start with a few and build your arsenal over time. Soon you'll be set for any dish, occasion or season in style. Antique serving pieces in modern shapes add heirloom chic to a buffet. And don't be shy about repurposing: use a fancy fish knife to dish up lasagna. Or a sterling silver meat fork to spear-and-scoop trifles.

FISH FORK

OLIVE/ PICKLE FORK

MASTER BUTTER KNIFE

SAUCE LADLE

SOUP LADLE

SALAD SERVERS

SERVING
SPOON

PIE
SERVER

MEAT
FORK

CARVING
KNIFE

CARVING
FORK

SHARPENING
STEEL

THINK INSIDE THE BOX

Full sets of anything are always more costly than separates, and flatware is no exception. Get creative and curate your own collection in smaller batches—six spoons here, another six there—until your set is complete. Stick to simpler materials and patterns that play well together. Then store your flatware in an empty silverware chest—their troves are often sold separately, leaving sturdy wooden boxes at next-to-nothing flea market prices. After a quick coat of paint, even the most mumsy silverware chest deserves a gold medal for glamour, so leave it out. A piece like this is too pretty to put away.

TRANSFORM A SILVERWARE CHEST into a dazzling storage piece with spray paint.

MATERIALS

- Painter's Tape
- Newspaper
- Sandpaper
- Zinsser Primer Spray
- Spray Paint (Valspar makes some of the best colors I've seen.)

STEP ONE: Remove hardware. **STEP TWO:** Cover the inside surfaces with paper and tape to secure in place, **STEP THREE:** Sand lightly. **STEP FOUR:** Prime with Zinsser spray in a well-ventilated area; let dry. **STEP FIVE:** Spray paint in a color that works for you; let dry. **STEP SIX:** Replace hardware.

A TIGHT COLOR
PALETTE OF FLOWERS
CREATES A NO-FAIL
ARRANGEMENT.
HERE THE HOT PINK
HYACINTHS AND
PARROT TULIPS IN A
LAVENDER WEDGWOOD
VASE MAKE A BOLD
STATEMENT.

I ADDED THIS VINTAGE BRASS MIRROR TO MY BUTLER'S PANTRY ON WHEELS, GIVING IT AN INDUSTRIAL GLAM VIBE IN THE KITCHEN AT PINE HILL.

HOT WHEELS

If you want to create gorgeous tables, buffets and parties that will give your guests something to remember, you're going to need stuff—and stuff always needs a home when you're not making magic with it. As you curate your arsenal of essential serving pieces and accessories, find stylish storage solutions that work hard, like this utility cart from Lowe's that I turned into a butler's pantry on wheels. After lining the drawers with felt, I filled it with all of the items I use the most. The cart's cool, industrial vibe creates a surprising addition in the kitchen at Pine Hill and ensures that everything I need for entertaining guests stays stylishly close at hand. Acrylic dividers from the Container Store keep table accessories neat and organized.

LOOK FOR LITTLE DISHES IN UNUSUAL SHAPES AND STYLES TO ADD A FINISHING TOUCH TO TABLES. FILL THEM WITH NUTS OR CANDIES IN COORDINATING COLORS.

CAKE PEDESTALS

Cake pedestals set the stage for dramatic desserts, garnering rave reviews for presentation. I was a newbie stylist when I picked up this pearl: put anything on a pedestal and it's the fast track to chic. I keep a stockpile of cake pedestals in different materials, but these are the types I go to time and again to give tables and buffets a stylish perch.

LOOK FOR CAKE PEDESTALS IN GRADUATED SIZES TO CREATE ARCHITECTURAL TOWERS. I MADE THIS SEE-THROUGH CENTERPIECE WITH THREE PRESSED GLASS CAKE PEDESTALS AND TWO TYPES OF CUPS—ANTIQUE CRYSTAL PUNCH AND MODERN GOLD ESPRESSO—FILLED WITH FLOWERS FROM COSTCO.

CAKE PEDESTALS AREN'T JUST FOR CAKE! GIVE A LIFT TO SANDWICHES AT LUNCH, HORS D'OEUVRES AT COCKTAIL HOUR OR FRUIT ALL THE TIME. EXTRA CREDIT: FOR A TOUCH OF GLAMOUR, STACK TIERED CAKE STANDS WITH JEWELRY AND COSMETICS ON A DRESSER OR VANITY.

STEELY WONDER

If you find your curated essentials growing into full-blown collections, carve out a corner for storage in a spare room, a garage or an attic. Assemble heavy-duty steel shelves and organize wares by color and type. Hang cups, soup bowls and small pitchers from S-hooks to save space.

DINNERWARE

Vintage plates with patterns have backgrounds that are usually either white or cream. Collect a set of each in a simple style to form the foundation for creating modern-mix table settings. The white set is from Christmas Tree Shops and the cream set is vintage Wedgwood Edme.

CREAM is as blank a canvas as *WHITE*.

DIY FELT PROTECTORS

Pop open a bottle of wine and pick up your pinking shears. Here's an easy project in the kitchen to keep dishes and serving pieces in tip-top shape, using plate pads and pouches you make yourself. Shear responsibly.

MATERIALS

- Felt
- Straight pins
- Scissors or pinking shears
- Stapler

PADS

STEP ONE: Cut felt into squares a little wider than your plates. **STEP TWO:** Pin four pieces together to save time. **STEP THREE:** Trace the outline of your plates onto the felt. **STEP FOUR:** Cut out the circles with the scissors or shears.

POUCHES

STEP ONE: Cut felt into strips a little wider than your serving pieces. **STEP TWO:** Fold them up and trim to size. **STEP THREE:** Staple the edges.

GLASSWARE

Curate a collection of cocktail glasses in colors, materials and motifs that suit your style. Here are the basics, *from top right:* **ALL-PURPOSE** glasses are always apropos for water and red and white wine. **FLUTES** keep the fizz in champagne cocktails; shorter styles are equally as chic as the tall ones. **COUPES** have wide rims and a speakeasy vibe, best for boozy drinks. **OLD-FASHIONED** (or rocks or lowball) glasses hold pours of dark liquors neat or over ice. **HIGHBALL** glasses are mostly for mixed drinks; swizzle sticks add personality. **WHITE WINE** glasses are smaller, keeping the wine chilled longer. **RED WINE** glasses have wide, full bowls to detect the nose of the wine and give it air.

DECANTERS

Leave it to the Venetians to dream up the decanter, blowing glass into slender-necked vessels with wide bodies for aerating wine. I'll decant just about anything I can—water at dinner, mixers at parties, iced tea all the time. Sometimes I even use a decanter to hold spring branches. Look for clean lines, graceful shapes and assorted sizes that work together.

IF YOU DIG A DECANTER BUT IT'S MISSING A STOPPER, BUY IT ANYWAY. CHANCES ARE, YOU'LL FIND ANOTHER STOPPER ALONG THE WAY OR ONLINE. JUST MAKE SURE YOU KNOW YOUR DIMENSIONS.

PITCHERS

Pick up a few pitchers (or jugs or creamers) in different sizes and shapes. Bigger sizes are better for water on a table or mixers on a bar, smaller ones for sauces and salad dressings. If you find an antique that's chipped or cracked, try camouflaging its flaws with flowers.

BAR EQUIPMENT

Get your party on with these containers, tools and other trappings of the well-equipped bar.

- Bar tray
- Ice Bucket
- Cocktail pitcher and stirrer
- Decanters
- Cocktail shaker
- Jigger
- Corkscrew
- Bottle opener
- Swizzle sticks
- Cocktail napkins
- Small bowls for garnish
- Tongs
- Cocktail picks

LOOK FOR FIGURAL BOTTLES. THEY MAKE A WHIMSICAL STATEMENT ON A BAR CART OR TRAY.

PEPPER MILLS

Pick up a few pepper mills in silver or brass for the table, and leave the chunky wooden types for cooking in the kitchen. Even if your spices are always spot-on, a pretty mill on the table lends European elegance—and it's easy to understand why: Peugeot of France invented the first pepper mill in 1842 and still makes some of the best today. Be sure to remove salt and pepper from the table before serving dessert—it's a rule of etiquette that shouldn't be broken.

CHARGER PLATES

Chargers aren't to be used for food, but they do add a decorative underlayer, catch splatters and protect surfaces from hot plates. Although they come in all sorts of materials, start with one set each in silver and brass (opt for real metal if you can, but a good finish on plastic is fine, too). Keep a third set on hand in a color that goes with your china. Use them for casual and formal occasions whenever you want to make a table feel fuller or more finished.

PLACE CARD HOLDERS

Pipe down, Miss Bossy Pants, and let your place cards do the talking. That way, you'll skip the last-minute scramble, putting everyone at the table—and you—more at ease. Look for place cards in different styles (casual, formal, whimsical) and use them to take the guesswork out of seating your guests.

SALTCELLARS

Salt's ability to season and preserve food spawned a slew of vessels called cellars. Styles ranged from bare bones to bling until in 1911, when the Morton Girl rained on the parade with salt that flowed freely from shakers. Add a pinch of glamour to the table with cellars and spoons in silver, gold, glass and stone, like fancy jewels for the table.

GOURMET SALTS

infuse cocktails and tabletops with exotic flair. Here are my faves:

- **FLEUR DE SEL** Delicate, glistening, mild. The perfect finishing salt for the table.

- **PINK HIMALAYAN** Dry and intense in shades of white, pink and deep red. Lovely on the rims of margaritas.

- **BLACK LAVA** Activated charcoal crystals with obsidian luster. Dramatic anywhere.

- **SMOKED** Woodsy and aromatic in owl grays and rich browns. A must on the Bloody Mary bar.

- **LEMON FLAKE** Bright, pungent, candy-sweet. A citrusy lift for the rim of a summer beer.

CANDLESTICKS

Pick up a few candlesticks in different styles and materials—they're the true mood-setters for any occasion. Think tall; think short; think everything in between. Pairs have their place, but singles have more fun. Not every candelabra will have you lighting up like Liberace—look for clean-lined styles in silver and brass.

CANDLES

Colorful candles update antique candlesticks in an instant. Keep an assortment on hand in a palette that appeals to you—bright and cheerful, demure and mysterious, soft and romantic. From the foyer to the backyard, formal dinners to casual get-togethers, colorful candles add a pop of personality.

ETERNAL FLAME Candles come in a variety of shapes, sizes and styles to suit everyone's taste. Natural beeswax burns cleaner than paraffin, a by-product of petroleum. Poured candles are the most common; hand-dipped burn longer and more beautifully. You pay for quality, but it's often worth the extra cost. Here are a few types to spark your inspiration:

- **ROLLED BEESWAX** candles burn clean and dripless with a light, honey scent. Favorite source: totallyhandmadebeeswaxcandles.com.

- **TAPERS** add drama. Twisted styles lend a vintage vibe; squares and obelisks are more modern. Favorite source for pillars, votives and hand-dipped tapers: creativescandles.com.

- **FIGURAL** candles lend whimsy all year long. Favorite source for specialty styles and shapes: greentreehomecandle.com.

- **FLOATING** candles and peonies in pressed glass compotes make a no-fail centerpiece.

- **PILLARS** illuminate hurricanes indoors and out.

- **NATURE-INSPIRED** candles with a faux bois finish or coral shapes are sculptural and unexpected.

- **VOTIVES** add a low layer of light to bars, buffets and tables.

OUR FRIENDS AT CREATIVE CANDLES IN KANSAS CITY HAND-DIP EVERY ONE OF THESE TAPERS. THEY'RE MY GO-TO SOURCE FOR COLORFUL CANDLES!

CANDLELIGHT makes everything better—all the flaws go away.

CURATE *OBJECTS*

Make a room feel more like you with objects that give it the finishing touch.

Styling houses for magazines, I've seen more than a few bare bookshelves, coffee tables and fireplace mantels. Even if everything else in a room comes together beautifully, it's that final layer of accessories that's often the most daunting. But you can find things that will infuse every bit of your personality into a room without spending a fortune if you simply take the time to look.

BOXES

Jewelry boxes as big as treasure chests were fashionable must-haves of 17th-century elites. But you don't have to be Marie Antoinette to see the beauty and utility in a decorative box. Styles abound, so find a piece that speaks to you and give it new life. I use the Italian mosaic box in the center for holding remote controls on the coffee table. The brass shell jewelry box now holds pushpins on a desk.

LOOK FOR UNUSUAL SHAPES AND PAY ATTENTION TO MARKINGS. ITALIAN JEWELRY DESIGNER ELSA PERETTI DESIGNED THIS ONE IN THE SHAPE OF A BEAN FOR HALSTON IN THE '70S.

DECORATIVE BOWLS

Oversized bowls in eye-catching patterns capture the spotlight wherever they go. Place a decorative bowl on the center of a dining table, or plant one in the foyer for catching keys, cell phones and leashes. Even solids make a statement with floating peonies or fresh fruit. Blue-and-white patterns are classic good taste; birds make my heart sing. Size is what's important, so look for bowls that catch your eye—and go big.

CURIOSITIES

Eccentric objects are the real personalities in a room—and the most fun to find. Unusual things lend an offbeat sensibility that can be playful, whimsical or chic. Layering in figurative objects like busts and statues is one of the best ways to animate a room. But you don't always have to buy something new to get a polished look. Take an object you already have in a great shape but a ho-hum finish, spray-paint it matte black and it instantly looks like Wedgwood basalt. Listen to your instincts here: if an object stops you in your tracks, or makes you laugh along the way, buy it.

GINGER JARS

There's nothing creepy about a ginger jar in a room, especially if it's full of life, like flowering quince branches. Take a cue from Gloria Vanderbilt and arrange a collection of jars on wall brackets. Pairs look splendid flanking a mirror in an entryway. New styles can be just as striking as vintage.

HIDE STEMS IN OPAQUE VASES. FOR AN EASY SUMMER ARRANGEMENT, I'LL FILL THIS MERCURY GLASS TRUMPET WITH VARIEGATED HOSTAS FROM THE GARDEN.

VASES

Flowers don't have to be pricey to look polished. The right container can turn inexpensive blooms into custom bouquets. Start by curating a collection of vessels in traditional shapes. Then, in the next chapter, learn how to mix in unusual containers.

- TRUMPETS flair, creating exuberant sprays.

- CYLINDERS have straight sides for flowers with unusual shapes and graceful tilts.

- SPHERES create lush globes of flowers.

- BOTTLES narrow at the top for single stems and branches.

- LOW PANS and bowls call for floating flowers.

- PAILS give freedom to big blooms and bunches.

The color of a front door introduces guests to the world inside. I personalized ours by painting it a deep indigo blue that feels fresh, inviting and a little mysterious.

Make an entrance with *ATTITUDE* guests won't soon forget.

For years I never missed a Sunday at church. At least that's what my friend Deborah and I called it every time we'd make our early morning pilgrimage to the Chelsea Flea Market. I met Deborah when I was working as the senior decorating editor at *Martha Stewart Living*, where every day I'd sit through meetings, perusing Pantone chips in assorted shades of greige. It was a subdued, tone-on-tone aesthetic I'd once embraced, but even if the spark of bold color had come into my eyes styling a shoot, I wouldn't have dared deliver props that strayed from the magazine's vision.

After meeting Deborah at an event she hosted at her former antiques store Buck House in Carnegie Hill, we exchanged remarks about our shared addiction to treasure hunting, a lack of storage space, etc., and promptly began to enable one another every chance we got. While I went digging in boxes at the flea market for china, silver and glass, she shopped for a sophisticated mix of items in colorful combinations.

Stepping into Deborah's living room for drinks one night, I felt like an awestruck Dorothy opening the door to a dazzling Technicolor Oz. Exotic prints in vibrant hues splashed like brushstrokes around the room, animating windows, upholstery and pillows. The settee was French, the rug Chinese Deco and the lamps Italian Brutalist. It was a heady mix that for years would float in and out of my mind. I was on the edge of my seat when Deborah returned from the kitchen holding a brass and enamel tray with a pair of goblets in the most spellbinding shade of blue.

After appearing on Bravo's *Top Design* and starting a blog with Jaithan, I left my position at *Martha Stewart Living* and moved out of the city in favor of greener pastures upstate. In a 1760s farmhouse, we started decorating rooms, setting tables for the blog and producing freelance stories for magazines. Finally, I had a laboratory in which to begin my own journey into personal style.

Then came the opportunity to design a table unlike any other I had before. It was for an event called "A Date

INSTAGRAM MOMENT: I FOUND THIS HEAVY ITALIAN DOOR KNOCKER IN THE BASEMENT AT AN ESTATE SALE. NOW IT ADDS A BIT OF PARK AVENUE ATTITUDE TO THE FRONT DOOR AT PINE HILL FARM.

with a Plate," benefiting a community's local charities. A trip to a barn sale sparked my inspiration; there I found a set of Wedgwood bowls with vivid flowers growing wildly up the sides. Although it was an antique English pattern, the palette felt fresh, with pink, turquoise and yellow hues. A solid cloth in any of these colors would have made a pretty table, but standing in the aisles of a fabric outlet, faced with the glorious freedom of choosing for only myself, I wanted more than pretty. I wanted to create something truly original that reflected my style. With a bright pink-and-orange ikat from Quadrille, I returned home to experiment with a new kind of mix.

After turning the fabric into a trio of runners, I pulled other elements in measured steps. To give the eye a break between the patterned bowls and runners, I layered in white porcelain plates from Christmas Tree Shops and vintage brass chargers from a thrift store. For the flatware, I combined gold-plated mid-century spoons and forks with antique mother-of-pearl knives I'd found at a pawn shop. While the ikat gave the table energy, it needed a jolt of cool to temper the tropical vibe. I considered the pattern on the bowls—pink peonies sprouting from leaves in the most spellbinding blue. Quickly I picked up the phone, dialed Deborah at home and asked to borrow six of her splendid blue opaline goblets. I carried the color into napkins, candles, candies and, for a fashionable touch, bohemian chic earrings from Target that I turned into napkin rings. That table setting proved to be our most popular blog post yet and inspired the title of this book as well. Finally, I'd found my own path into an expressive style that felt more like me, and I've never looked back.

Now that you've discovered some of my favorite things to look for, where to find them and how to restore them, in this chapter you'll harness the power of color and pattern to infuse your finds with soul. I'll show you how to mix china, linens, flatware and glass to create extraordinary table settings with confidence. You'll learn to combine vintage and new textiles, trims and bed linens in exciting, colorful ways. These are the tools you'll use time and again to design every room, table setting and party that celebrates your style.

MIX *DECORATING*

Summon the confidence to create bold combinations that bring you joy.

I see a lot of rooms—on blogs and Instagram, in portfolios and scouting shots—and it's always the personal statements that stop me in my scroll, draw me in and entrance me with a captivating mix of color and pattern, time periods and materials. The schemes are never any particular palette or style; the furniture could as easily be Hepplewhite or IKEA hack; and the art and objects tell personal stories. But the one element these rooms—and their inhabitants—share is confidence. Stylish things can be found anywhere. If you buy only the things that bring you joy, a room will always feel right.

WHEN IT COMES TO
DECORATING, COLOR
THEORY IS FULL OF DOS
AND DON'TS. MY ADVICE:
START WITH SOMETHING
YOU LOVE—A FLOWER,
A FABRIC SWATCH, A
BRACELET, A SPOON—AND
CREATE A MIX THAT MAKES
YOU HAPPY.

TEXTILES & TRIMS

PLAY WITH PILLOWS They are an easy and inexpensive way to have fun with pattern and test your tolerance for mixing prints. The more the better for me, but I do stick to a palette to pull a look together. Here, vivid needlepoint pillows adorn a neutral sofa. They're warm and cheery in the winter, cool and colorful in the summer. **TRIM IT OUT** Embellish vintage and new furniture, curtains, lampshades, pillows and tablecloths with ribbon to get a custom look without the cost. For instance, find a pair of lamps at a flea market, then pick up shades at Target and trim them with ribbon in a color that works in your decor. **CUT AND SEW** When on the road, always try to sneak in a spin through local

thrift shops. A chair might not fit in the overhead bin (believe me, I've tried), but you can certainly take home vintage textiles in a suitcase. Look for fabrics in a mix of colors and patterns you like and use them for small projects with big personality—pillows, a slipcover on an upholstered headboard or a topper for a floor-length tablecloth. **MIX PATTERNS** Coordinating patterns isn't as hard as you might think. Start with a statement print that's big on color, like this allover marbleized fabric. Carry some of the colors over to another pattern; here, it's the large-scale paisley. Repeat a color again in a smaller scale pattern. The solid gives the eye a rest, while turquoise trim ties them all together.

LOOK FOR A MIX OF
BEDDING THAT CARRIES
A PALETTE THROUGH.
HERE, A VINTAGE PLAID
PILLOWCASE AND A
NEW, TRIMMED SHAM
ECHO THE YELLOW OF
THE DUVET.

DREAM SEQUENCE

Rekindle the spark in your bedding with a lively mix of color
and pattern. Pair solids with stripes, plaids with florals—and if
you're feeling really frisky—combine them all together. Too wild?
Start here: buy two solid sets and mix them together. After
you become more confident, create other looks by layering in
white sheets with colored trims. Go all the way with vintage
pillowcases in playful patterns.

FROM GOODWILL TO GLAM
Jaithan and I were doing one of our routine spins through the Goodwill near our apartment when he found this bamboo and rattan étagère from the '70s in perfect condition. But as much as I love spilling secrets over cheesecake, I wanted a look that's more glam than Golden Girls. With gold metallic tape, I wrapped every joint of the étagère, giving it a high-end sheen in less than an hour. Repeat even the simplest update, like swapping out old hardware on furniture, and it can make a huge difference.

FOILED AGAIN
Guests should see your personality shine, too. In our spare room in the city, the étagère I updated with gold foil tape takes the place of a bedside table. Going vertical frees up floor space, creates storage and affords plenty of opportunities to display books, objects and other oddities. The chrome-and-brass headboard is a thrift shop find; the bedding combines vintage and new linens. Now guests have a room with a vibrant mix that makes them feel welcome.

LOOK FOR ART IN DIFFERENT MEDIAS AND SIZES, ALONG WITH CONTRASTING FRAMES THAT SPEAK TO YOU. HERE I LAYERED A LARGE DECOUPAGE ABSTRACT PIECE, A MODERN NEEDLEPOINT, AND A SCREEN PRINT OF POLO HORSES.

TWO UPDATES

added new life to thrift shop finds. *Top*: The parsons chair was a solid piece with good lines. At Calico, I found a gorgeous chartreuse velvet, and for less than $400, I have a custom chair that's totally my style. *Bottom*: This chinoiserie brass hardware was an estate sale snag; four of the corners went onto a bamboo chest from the Goodwill for a boho vibe.

TO GIVE MY PEACOCK FIREPLACE MANTLE MORE PLUMAGE, I USED GOLD METALLIC TAPE, TRIMMING THE CORNERS WITH AN X-ACTO KNIFE. USE IT ON CHAIRS, BOOKCASES AND CABINETS TO ADD DECORATOR BLING.

HARD CANDY

In the office of our New York apartment, *opposite*, color and pattern collide in a high-octane mix of furniture, textiles, art and objects. Nearly every element in the room, from the chinoiserie screen down to the blue opaline bowl, was purchased secondhand at flea markets, thrift shops, estate sales and online marketplaces like Craigslist. The vintage kilim rug inspired the palette, its hard-candy colors punctuating artwork, books and blooms. I bought the brass plaque with a fish at Brimfield and hung it over the brick in a non-working fireplace.

MAGIC MANTLE

The painted mantle anchoring the room sets the stage for a series of still lifes that are anything but stagnant. Since I'm always finding new treasures to love, I'll change up art and artifacts often for a whole new look. *Above*, art and nature interweave in a living, shifting mix that blends materials and motifs in curious combinations. I found the hand-painted chinoiserie screen at an estate sale. The painted marbleized disc is by Arthur McViccar.

A cloisonné vase enameled with a chinoiserie dragon holds an untamed mix of ranunculus, cosmos, scabiosas and hellebores. A Lucite bracket gives it a light-as-a-feather perch.

MIX *FLOWERS*

Pair containers and blooms in surprising combinations.

Mondays during the summer with Pop-pop were the best. That's when we'd go into the house on the estate where he worked, gather up containers and clip blooms in the cutting garden. There was a special container for each room, and every one of them we'd fill with leaves and flowers that changed in the same magical way as the garden. My favorite was a foot bath on the dining table covered in pink peonies. Pop-pop told me it came all the way from China. We'd stuff it with roses in bright colors and then when the leaves turned, we used those instead. These days, I bring flowers from the country to the city, picking up roses from Costco on the way. I'll still fill up my vases and other vessels with a changing mix of greenery and blooms that bring nature's magic home.

A CONTAINER BY ANY OTHER NAME

Vases are classic containers for flowers and foliage, so once you've curated your favorites, add in a few oddballs, too. *Top left:* You don't have to go big to make an impact. Take a tiny vessel in an unusual style or shape and create a luxurious mix. Here, a black glass grenade sets off a ladylike medley of garden roses, ranunculus, daffodils and checkered lilies. A marble box gives it gravitas. *Top right:* Contrasting styles between a vessel and its blooms create interest: a decidedly formal silver-plated pitcher holds a casual mix of pink and burgundy peonies, silver dollar eucalyptus and sensitive ferns from my garden. *Bottom left:* This container is more of a girl gone wild. It's actually a brass ice bucket in the form of a pineapple with its top off. Flowers in different shapes, tones and textures arranged naturally carry the fruit's organic motif from vessel to blooms, creating a cohesive look that's sculptural and a bit imperfect.

LOOK FOR FLOWERS AND GREENERY IN A VARIETY OF COLORS AND TEXTURES—COARSE, CRINKLY, RUFFLED, FINE—FOR A MORE NATURAL MIX.

PERFECTLY IMPERFECT

Creative friends help open our eyes to new ideas. So when Melissa and Addison Searles of Twigss in northern California came to town, we decided to catch up over—what else?—champagne and flowers at *chez moi*. In a vintage Lucite ice bucket from the bar, we made this bright, casual arrangement of cosmos, ranunculus, hellebores and jasmine. We kept the palette of the blooms tonal, varying sizes and textures to create an imperfect mix that feels right at home.

A FLOWER ARRANGER'S KIT

You don't need to be a pro to make arrangements that make you happy. With a few essential supplies, your inner florist can finally bloom.

- **FLORAL SHEARS** Trims soft stems, excess greenery and spent blooms. I like Sakagen.

- **BYPASS PRUNERS** Cuts tough-stemmed flowers and woody growth.

- **UTILITY LIGHTER** Some flowers (like poppies and poinsettias) release a milky sap that clogs other stems. Sear their tips over an open flame for about 30 seconds to seal in the sap each time you cut them.

- **FROGS** Keep stems in vessels too wide or shallow firmly in place. Can be vintage or new in materials such as metal, ceramic or glass. Spiky types hold up thin, slender stems; frogs with holes anchor thicker stems.

- **WIRE** Can bundle stems so they're easier to arrange.

- **ADHESIVE** Secures frogs in containers. Remove sticky residue with mayonnaise or Goo Gone.

- **KNIFE** Any knife with a short blade and good edge can be used to cut stems and carve floral foam.

- **FLORAL FOAM** Dense, water-absorbent anchor for supporting stems in arrangements.

- **TAPE** Supports stems in a grid across the opening of a container. Use white or dark floral tape, depending on the vessel, and household cellophane for glass.

- **SCISSORS** One for cutting sticky things like putty and tape; another for ribbon and paper. Mark the handles with a Sharpie.

- **STEM STRIPPER:** Removes thorns and leaves—a must for roses.

EXTRA CREDIT: GARNISH A TRAY OF HORS D'OEUVRES WITH A SINGLE BLOOM ANCHORED IN A TINY FROG. SECURE IT IN PLACE WITH FLORAL PUTTY.

MIX *TABLEWARE*

Throw open the cupboards and get ready to rethink your table.

Change inspires new ways of looking at old things. So as you start changing up colors, patterns, materials and motifs in your home, extend them to the table, to the patio or to anywhere else where friends and family can gather to share in your creativity. Mixing vintage and new tableware into what you already own doesn't have to be expensive or time-consuming. For instance, you can freshen up a set of wedding china with forks from a flea market, jewel-toned goblets from the Goodwill or colorful salad plates from West Elm. Tastes change—and so should we.

SURFACE MATTERS

Plates and platters that add fresh life to tables can be as new or old, simple or elaborate as you'd like. Coalport plates made in 1830, with lush, allover blooms contrast with Kate Spade's matte black plates faceted like prisms. The colors and patterns of these pieces form infinite combinations, each with its own style—its own story. Create an alluring mix on a table and tell yours.

ONE FORK, FIVE WAYS

Once you've curated a set of flatware with simple patterns, it's easy to change the look on a table with linens. *Clockwise from top:* Monogrammed homespun evokes a charming country retreat. Vintage Vera feels color-me-retro. Nautical ropes are seaside chic. Peacock-y blue boasts classic cool. And an Art Deco monogram says uptown glam. If you keep your go-to flatware stylish but simple, then your personality shines with linens.

COLORFAST *Keep one variable constant and vary the others. Here, a vintage basketweave tablecloth sets the scene for a summery blue-and-yellow buffet, mixing platters in different time periods and patterns.*

ONE PLATE, THREE LOOKS

You can never go wrong with blue and white—it's a classic color combo that works in every season. You know the drill: white tablecloth + blue-and-white china + blue napkins + silver flatware + clear glasses + leafy centerpiece. It all adds up to a mix that's pretty but by no means unique. Here, I offer up three looks with a single transferware plate, combining it with napkins, flatware, glasses, cellars and shakers to create place settings with a modern mix. Repetition is power: it can give even the most peculiar element purpose. So as you dive deeper into each place setting, picture them en masse—down a rectangle, around a circle—producing a sum far greater than its parts. There will always be the pretty types two steps from a snorefest. Reimagine ol' blue to create something fresh and original.

LADYLIKE LUXE

Tablecloths in solid colors are safe, but a spirited pattern can infuse even the most traditional china with new life. Find a fabric with at least one hue that relates to your plate (here, it's blue) and use the rest of the palette as a guide, varying tones and textures for a modern mix. If contrasting patterns are too much for you, slip a charger between tablecloth and plate, like an intermezzo for a meal.

TABLECLOTH A stylized floral brings fresh color and a painterly feel to the mix, creating a backdrop with a dense, allover pattern that complements, not competes with, the plate.

NAPKIN A brass-and-enamel napkin ring from the '70s encircles an antique hemstitched napkin I dip-dyed a pale shade of pink inspired by the fabric.

BREAD PLATE *Bread plates take up space, but they bring an element of surprise. To give the mix edge, I added a modernist bread plate with a quirky Asian-style monogram.*

GLASSWARE *Twin stems adorn goblets for water and wine—one is citron vaseline glass from Portieux Vallerysthal, the other is cobalt blue.*

FLATWARE *Gold-toned flatware gives the mix glamour. The knife and spoon are plated; the fork is brass bamboo. Each piece is shaped gracefully, with patterns that play well together.*

SALT & PEPPER *Salt and pepper cellars pair with spoons in contrasting styles and lavish materials such as gold, sterling silver and mother-of-pearl.*

EURO CLASH

Layering china in contrasting styles can update a dinner plate just as beautifully. Here, a salad plate from Royal Copenhagen in a stylized floral motif gives the place setting a graphic edge. The patterns on both the dinner and salad plates are vintage, but the two together add up to a modern mix with Scandinavian cool. Wintry sunset hues in the fabric bestow a moody glow, inspiring the table's ethereal palette of amethyst, silver and gunmetal gray.

LINENS I paired a crisp gray napkin from Tag with a silk-and-linen woven from Gray Line Linen. Fringe trim takes a walk on the wild side—with or without a napkin ring.

FLATWARE The bone-handle knife is German; the spoon and fork are from France, where it's tradition to monogram utensils on the backs, and to set the table with the flatware facing down so the monograms are visible.

GLASSWARE Amethyst goblets from the '40s add jewel-toned shimmer to smoked gray glasses from the '70s. Transparent stems tie the two together.

SALT & PEPPER Details make the mix: a cranberry-red saltcellar with an ivory spoon brings depth to the palette, while a silver-plated pepper grinder echoes the European feel of the flatware.

SAFARI SLEEK

These organic materials and motifs might look like a misfit for the blue-and-white plate, but they give it a prominence that, if repeated with confidence, would send its watery blues straight to the Sahara. The effect is well suited to fall, with an inviting blend of natural textures punctuated with sleek accents and handmade touches. The animal print is a cotton blend from Calico. The bread plate is the saucer to a Paris Porcelain teacup; the knife is German with a brass blade.

NAPKIN A keystone napkin ring from Pier 1 Imports lends a modern organic note to an antique napkin with a hand-embroidered monogram.

GLASSWARE Black and gold glassware gives the table Versace sheen. The water glasses are King's Crown thumbprint; the wine goblets are Italian cased glass.

FLATWARE Utensils blend rough and refined, natural and man-made: the handle of the knife is wood, the fork staghorn and the spoon brass.

SALT & PEPPER I paired a porcelain pepper shaker with a chinoiserie saltcellar, tying them together with gilded details. The salt spoon is '60s Lucite.

MIX MASTER

Everyone has a weakness for one thing or another. Mine is dishes, glasses, flatware and linens. These are the key to creating place settings with an exuberant mix of colors, patterns, time periods and materials. To illustrate easy ways of mixing china, here are six combinations both separately and together as they would appear on a table. Start with something you already own—chargers, your wedding china, a set of bowls from the flea market— and use the ideas here to inspire you.

THE ELEMENTS: Brass charger + Ironstone dinner plate + Pink band service plate + Chinoiserie soup bowl + Blue lusterware bread plate.

THE MIX: Feminine and formal—an uptown lady decorator with a thing for chintz.

YOU'RE INVITED: To a spring birthday dinner with other ladylike types.

LOOK FOR: China and chargers in octagon shapes; layer them in with round for bad-girl points.

THE ELEMENTS: Coalport dinner plate + Paris Porcelain salad plate + Shell service plate + Victorian bouillon cup.

THE MIX: Fresh and pretty with a pay off—soup, salad, surprise!

YOU'RE INVITED: To an elegant seaside soirée.

LOOK FOR: China in unusual shapes or textures (here, the shell plates).

THE ELEMENTS: Kate Spade dinner plate + German pierced porcelain salad plate + Royal Doulton soup cup and saucer.

THE MIX: Midnight garden—trellis-y plates over black stoneware pair good and evil to beguiling effect.

YOU'RE INVITED: To an autumnal dinner with a warming soup to start.

LOOK FOR: Plates with decorative openwork to layer over solids.

LOOK FOR SETS OF SALAD/DESSERT PLATES IN UNUSUAL SHAPES, MODERN AND TRADITIONAL PATTERNS, AND DIFFERENT MATERIALS. THIS WILL ALLOW YOU TO CREATE TABLE SETTING MIXES THAT HAVE THEIR OWN PERSONALITY FOR WHATEVER THE OCCASION MIGHT BE.

THE ELEMENTS: Sascha B dinner plate + Italian salad plates + Green-band service plate + Gold-handled soup bowl + Malachite-print bread plate.
THE MIX: Classic rock—antiquity meets geology.
YOU'RE INVITED: To Italian night. Let's just hope Teresa is a no-show.
LOOK FOR: China with natural motifs.

THE ELEMENTS: White charger + French Bon Vivant plate + Hand-painted salad plate + Pink lusterware bread plate.
THE MIX: All eyes on her—an A-list star with plain-Jane backup and a sizzling sideshow.
YOU'RE INVITED: To a boozy brunch.
LOOK FOR: Plates with asymmetrical patterns.

THE ELEMENTS: Haviland chargers + Polish dinner plate + Rosenthal salad plate + Majolica cabbage-leaf bowl.
THE MIX: Sophisticated whimsy—a kooky cabbage-leaf bowl cuts the formalities.
YOU'RE INVITED: To a fancy farm-to-table dinner.
LOOK FOR: Quirky elements to lighten the mood.

Pillows in a medley of colors, textures and patterns ensure the sofa at Pine Hill Farm is as lively for throwing cocktail parties as it is loungey for binge-watching Revenge by the fire.

There are two sides to every story—at least the provocative types—so the one you tell at home should be no exception. Unexpected combinations are the hallmark of a modern mix—pattern on pattern, vintage and new, simple and elaborate, rough with luxe. Oddball objects add character and surprises thicken the plot.

These days, my story is a tale of two places—an apartment in New York and a country house in Connecticut. Jealous? Don't be. Peel back the layers and you'll find modest rooms with an affordable mix of furniture, textiles, art, books and objects I bought one beloved treasure at a time.

In New York City, wealth courses through the real estate market faster than the 4 Express train from 125th to 14th Street. Down in SoHo, light streams through arched windows into airy lofts. On the Upper West Side, ornamental moldings encircle vast living rooms in prewar buildings. Up farther still, in townhouses near Columbia University, carved wood staircases climb to sun-drenched terraces. While across town, in a cookie-cutter condo clinging to Manhattan by a thread, Jaithan and I have assembled our own version of opulence. Crisp, white walls are the backdrop to a vibrant array of graphic and uplifting textiles. Secondhand steals mingle with retail deals in combinations that bring an upscale feel to affordable finds. Since the space is small and we entertain often, I keep decorative essentials like compotes, trays and platters on slim bookshelves so they're always within reach. The mix favors modern, pairing clean-lined furniture and curated serveware with a distinctly urban point of view.

When Friday comes around and the exodus east begins, Jaithan and I head north to a cozy 1930s cape in the Connecticut countryside. We call it Pine Hill Farm, named for the soaring trees on the property, where the late afternoon sun casts a radiant glow across the foothills of the Berkshires, up a grassy knoll and into our living room. Although the wild turkeys outside might scamper when they hear us pull in, inside the mix is anything but timid. Riotous, eye-popping prints cover curtains, pillows

INSTAGRAM MOMENT: OUR DRESSER ONCE BELONGED TO MY GRANDPARENTS. I DIDN'T DO A THING TO IT BUT STYLE THE TOP WITH A LAYERED MIX, MAKING IT MORE ME WITHOUT A FUSSY MAKEOVER.

and bed linens. Modern art enlivens knotty pine walls. A Greek bust rubs elbows with a chinoiserie lamp. And up in the attic, I keep my finds in a personal prop house, rotating them onto tables, bars, buffets and surfaces in every room as I travel my own course into style. Clutter is comfort in the country and objects tell stories. There's soul in the mix and you can feel it in everything.

The city and country might be physical places in these pages, but they're also points of view that can inspire a pillow, a tableau or even an entire room in your home, wherever you live. If you're more of a minimalist, try tipping the mix towards the city with spare shapes and modern materials, like Lucite and polished silver or brass. Shake up the monotony with a handmade textile, ornate wall sconces or antique barware. Curate your essentials with an editor's eye, assembling a versatile mix of serveware that works together for the way you entertain.

If more is more, take thee to the country, layering on colors, patterns and textures in bold gestures. Surround yourself with keepsakes that carry special meaning, whether found at a flea market or handed down from family. Take risks—if something doesn't work, change it. You can't expect to make a journey towards a more creative life without a few missteps along the way.

Whether it's the city, the country or a combination of the two that inspires your approach, be patient—the mix that truly captures you takes time. As entertaining as they are, reality design shows have little in common with real-life decorating. I wish Ty Pennington would show up at my door, cut a piece of ribbon and send me to a townhouse in the Village while my new neighbors cheered me on. A quick fix like spray paint can transform a piece of furniture in an instant, but it might take ten trips to the flea market before you find it—and ten happy car rides home with a trunk full of stuff! All those richly layered rooms in vintage magazines look collected over time because they were; old-school decorators were part of the family, refreshing furniture, swapping things in and out, traveling the world to give their clients something special. But you can easily create a chic, affordable mix of furniture, art and objects that's every bit as stylish—and personal—if you take the time to look.

STYLE *COUNTRY*

Paint a vibrant self-portrait that brings your home to life.

Here in the country, design is never done. It's an approach to decorating that's playful, personal and, above all, confident. Color and pattern create a happy rhythm. Heirloom antiques mix with retail steals. And beloved keepsakes paint a vibrant self-portrait that celebrates us. Everything that matters is here. In these walls, we find our sanctuary, our safe haven and our laboratory, where eccentricities thrive. There are no apologies for taste and no mistakes to mourn. There is only the joy of our never-ending journey into style.

ARTFUL RETREAT

At the outset of my own journey at Pine Hill, I was faced with dual challenges in the living room: preserve the character of its knotty pine walls, and infuse the room with a fresh spirit. A tree-of-life print from Duralee inspired bold curtains that elongate the room's height and spark its palette. Burnt orange hues pick up the knotty pine; steely blues enliven modernist art; and verdant greens bring the outdoors in. To throw country off-kilter, I added clean-lined furniture in Calico fabrics: the bench is covered in a stylish flame stitch; the chair is a city transplant. To display our treasures, I painted a slim pair of built-ins a bright coat of white.

WILD LIFE

If Diana Vreeland got hitched to Buffalo Bill, honeymooned in China and moved to Connecticut, this might be the garden in hell of their dreams—but it's ours! In the living room at Pine Hill, gilt details and riotous patterns in a rustic shell conjure English country cottage with uptown attitude. Solid fields in textural neutrals—knotty pine walls, a large sisal rug and a linen Eton sofa from Ballard Design—give visual rest. The cameo lamp was my grandmother's; I updated it with a white shade and metallic trim. The vintage hide was a gift from Jaithan's uncle. In the winter, the room is comfortable and cozy; in the summer, cool and fresh with a modern mix of treasures that tell *our* story. What will yours be?

One of my longtime mentors, iconic decorator Bunny Williams, gave me the Picasso floor lamp from her Beeline collection. The art is by Vivi Wheaton of Like William Studio.

LIBRARY HOURS

When it comes to furniture, sometimes all you want is a quick fix or a trendy touch so you buy a piece inexpensively, live with it for a while and move on. Other times, you invest money, time or a combination of the two to get something special—money for the stuff other people make by hand or time for the stuff you revamp yourself. Of course, those are the pieces you tend to keep. My grandfather restored this old pharmaceutical cabinet that I've carried from apartment to apartment to display china, wedged into a four seasons patio to store flower vessels, and turned into the bookcase, *above,* to hold magazines. Colorful pillows brighten the vintage sofa—and cocktails in the library—but unlike the permanence of a prized piece of furniture, these hues are easily here, then gone, making way for a new kind of mix.

LITTLE RED DRESS

Look high; buy low—that's my advice. Take the veneered dresser, *above,* that I found at a Goodwill. The door knocker hardware is what's golden—at least it was. I'd once seen a similar dresser with a lacquered exterior and drawers covered in grasscloth, but it wasn't in my budget. So with high gloss spray paint and a roll of grasscloth, I added color and texture to the dresser myself. Then I called in a pro to replate the brass and polish it to a high shine. The price I paid was still a fraction of the cost of the original. Now I have a piece that's one-of-a-kind, *right,* adding a blaze of color to the foyer's modern mix.

I found the Greek key chair at a flea market, painted it black, embellished it with a metallic gold pen and upholstered the seat myself in a Colonial Williamsburg toile. Our friend Ibie gave us the cross-stitch portrait of Jaithan and me by Carrie Burch of Stitch Folks.

LOOK FOR A MIX OF WARES IN COLORS AND MATERIALS THAT WORK IN YOUR KITCHEN. IF YOU HAVE OPEN SHELVES OR GLASS CABINETS, SHOW THEM OFF! SOMETIMES, THE MESSIER THE BETTER—JUST MAKE SURE THEY PLAY WELL TOGETHER.

PUFF, THE MAGIC SERVER

PUFF, THE MAGIC SERVER Flea markets are full of oddball items that may have once been must-haves but have since fallen out of fashion. Whenever I see something unusual but outdated, I try to imagine ways of giving it new life. Take this old pipe stand: as much as I love the idea of wearing a silk smoking jacket in the country, I preferred to reinvent the thing entirely. After a quick swipe of mineral oil to bring back its shine, I stuffed it with spoons, toast and soft-boiled eggs for a personalized server at breakfast.

CHARM SCHOOL

Here in the country, my kitchen is command central. The day starts with a fresh brew in gilded German shaving mugs and ends when the last salt spoons are dried and put away. The interior combines familiar and surprising elements in a modern mix: French-style chairs with a bohemian peacock chair; a beadboard backsplash with an Italian fish platter; bamboo blinds with a Lucite chandelier. When guests with little ones in tow stay the weekend, I set the table for a colorful breakfast, *opposite,* using a fancy but friendly mix of finds: grapefruit brûlée in antique champagne coupes for the adults, Lucky Charms in melon-shaped majolica bowls for the kids. The tie-dyed textile makes love, not war, with hand-painted dishes. Later, after antiquing around town, we'll reconvene in the kitchen, take our pick of glasses for cocktails, *above,* then head outside to watch the sun slip behind the pines.

FAR EAST FLAIR

Auntie Mame's dragon may have breathed fire at the door, but mine cast a spell of their own in the bedroom. They're printed on a vintage chinoiserie textile remnant in vivid colors—an unlikely pick for the walls but a just-right jolt of personality on the headboard. After padding a piece of plywood with batting, I attached it to the wall, stapled the fabric and finished the edges with trim. Then I borrowed its colors for a vibrant mix of bedding, combining patterns in tonal blues from indigo to sky punctuated with salmon-y pink. The diamond pattern shams are from Target; the paisley top sheet is vintage, shaking up the chinoiserie with a touch of prep.

STYLE *CITY*

Create fresh, opulent style on a budget.

What do you call a cookie-cutter condo in Upper Manhattan inhabited by a commitment phobe and a color fanatic? Jaithan and I call it home. In our East Harlem apartment, bright white walls are the backdrop to a rotating assemblage of clean-lined furniture, colorful textiles and curated collections. The mix is every bit as budget-friendly as that in the country, with surprising ideas you can easily steal to find your own style.

ONY DUQUETTE

VERS CAROLYNE ROEHM

UPTOWN MIX

In the living room a vibrant mix of color, pattern and texture enlivens a neutral sectional. It's an energizing space that brings together vintage textiles in a blue-and-green palette with pops of pink, persimmon and Popsicle red. Nothing is too permanent, so I change it up often, swapping out pillows and books for an entirely new look. Even the flowers, *left,* get the eclectic treatment, combining colors and textures in a Wedgwood basalt bowl outfitted with a glass flower frog to hold the blooms in place. I put the arrangement on a brass pedestal, giving it an air of importance and reflecting light onto the bowl's decorative relief.

LOOK FOR USED BOOKS ON AMAZON. IT'S A SMART WAY TO FILL A COFFEE TABLE. BUY THE SLIGHTLY WORN COPIES FOR EVEN MORE SAVINGS.

COVER GIRLS

I might break out in a cold sweat if Instagram doesn't update, but I'm really a bookworm at heart. So when it comes to my coffee table, I pile them on with stylish covers that make me happy. Dandy decorators and Hollywood starlets happen to be my muses, but anything goes, as long as it's pretty—and personalized. Even the IKEA Lack gets hacked with brass corners from decorativehardwarestudio.com, giving it a high-end look on a budget.

Pull favorite reads off bookshelves and onto a coffee or foyer table, then layer the scene with trays, boxes and other objects that capture your scholarly side. Small dishes and plates make one-of-a-kind coasters for coffee, cocktails and other liquid fuels.

David Hi... home...

DESIGNERS' OWN HOMES

ARCHITECTURAL DIGEST

AMERICAN STYLE

PATINA STYLE

THE NEW YORK TIMES SPANISH INTERIOR DECORATION

DECORATE

Laying the Elegant Table

ICANG...

MARIO

The Great Ameri...

BUNNIES

Eleanor Lambert

I SCORED A PAIR OF DANISH MODERN CHAIRS FOR $50 AT A SALVATION ARMY, SO I SPLURGED ON THIS BEACON HILL CURTAIN FABRIC IN ALL THE COLORS I WANTED TO USE IN THE ROOM.

ARTS & LETTERS

Art and books in a room can echo our lives—who we are, where we've been and what we love—louder than anything else. In the city, I arrange books on twin shelves leaving plenty of space for treasures that are both decorative and useful. The abstract painting that hangs between them is the work of our friend Anna Ullman of A.E.U. Studio. Her splashes of color infuse the beginning and end of this volume with the vibrant, playful spirit of a modern mix. The most pleasing art in a room is ultimately personal: look for artwork that reveals *you,* and style will always follow suit.

Call it my Valspar period: years back, I splattered this canvas with leftover house paint from a project. Here, it animates the wall over our bed and inspires the palette for the room. New canvases can be pricey—buy used ones at thrift shops, paint over them with white and channel your inner Kandinsky.

OLD SCHOOL

On a sliver of a wall just off the bedroom, *above right,* I display a prized gelatin print by the late photographer Slim Aarons, gifted to us by his daughter, Mary. An African beaded panther from a junk shop stands watch. In the hallway, *above,* a navy trellis print paper from Quadrille brings Palm Beach polish to a small dressing area outfitted with a modern wardrobe and an old-school brass valet with a shelf, *right,* for corralling cuff links and watches. The 1950s wrought iron X-bench is one of a pair covered in a fabric from Steve McKenzie.

TOP BRASS

Modern art meets traditional craft in our bedroom in the city. A basic chest of drawers from IKEA makes the chinoiserie lamp on top the star. It's a rummage sale find that I revamped with new brass feet (they're drawer knobs!) and a sleek black shade. Quilts can look old-fashioned, but this one lends homespun charm with colors that still feel fresh. The pillow is made from an old rug, adding a touch of antique to the mix.

WELL-DRESSED

Styling can be the fastest way to make inherited furniture feel more like you. The dresser in our bedroom, *opposite,* was part of a set my grandparents received as a wedding gift from their parents. I didn't do a thing to change it but style the top with lamps, artwork and objects, giving it personal style without a fussy makeover. New black shades on vintage lamps give the dresser an edge. Obelisks, grouped to make an impact, create a skyline with Roman grandeur. Every so often, I'll embellish them with costume jewelry for a more layered look. One of Jaithan's closest friends, Maryann Kenney, gifted him the sterling silver dish engraved with a K—an initial the two of them share.

BEFORE IT WAS MINE. Here is a picture of the dresser in my grandparents' first apartment.

LOOK FOR LAMPS THAT MAKE AN IMPACT. I FOUND THESE GREEN '80S LAMPS BASES AT A THRIFT SHOP, REWIRED THEM WITH A KIT AND FINISHED THEM OFF WITH MODERN DRUM SHADES.

Dusk settles over the apple orchard at Pine Hill Farm, as I put the finishing touches on a dinner party celebrating Jaithan's birthday. I always burn the tips of candles before guests arrive, so they'll light up fast when the time is right.

I wonder if things would have been different if Josiah Wedgwood had owned an iPhone. Or if Sascha Brastoff had known about Instagram. And what about Dorothy Thorpe? Would she have stopped twisting Lucite into pretzels to check Pinterest? This I know: if luminaries like these had let their online interactions get in the way of their offline creativity, a) my cupboards wouldn't have as much stuff, b) it would be a lot cheaper to move and c) styling parties wouldn't be half as fun!

The Victorians in 1900 knew all about stuff—and how to use it. Their social lives orbited around a front parlor, not a Facebook post. Upwardly mobile hosts greeted guests in well-appointed rooms before sitting down to tables decked out with a dizzying array of china, silver and glassware. In those days, clutter meant class—the more you had (and used!), the more well-to-do you looked. But as a tidal wave of conveniences swept through the century and tableware turned disposable, formal affairs faded to quick fixes. Why bother using the good stuff when you have to wash it by hand? Silver is such a chore; the crystal might break. And cloth napkins on the table? Not going to happen. Then it does happen (for an occasion "special" enough) and there comes a moment when you look across a table or a room glowing in candlelight, humming with laughter and think, *Why don't I do this more often?*

Parties are work, no matter how you look at them. They're fun, but they take effort. If you're hosting a cookout, sure, you can toss a few paper plates on a table, squeeze ketchup from the bottle and call it a day. But that's not my style. Nor is it yours, I suspect. If there's one thing I've learned over the years, it's that presentation matters. By pairing homemade favorites with store-bought shortcuts, you can free up precious time to create dazzling parties with a modern mix.

Cooking every dish from scratch can be a beautiful thing, and in culinary school I did. But by no means is it necessary to create a special experience for your guests. For instance, to throw a fun brunch that gets people involved, you could buy a bunch of quiches, make a delicious salad, then use your curated essentials

PICK A PITCHER FOR THE BAR THAT DOUBLES AS A FLOWER VESSEL WHEN YOU'RE NOT GETTIN' BOOZY WITH IT. THIS ONE IS ITALIAN CERAMIC FROM THE '60S WITH FRESH-CUT PEONIES.

to build a chic Bloody Mary bar with vintage pitchers, a mix of highball glasses and garnishes in different footed dishes and bowls. For an impromptu cocktail party, stash precut veggies in a compote with your favorite dip in a hollowed-out cabbage. Make one hors d'oeuvre yourself, then buy the rest and serve them all on platters in patterns that work together. And for a weekday dinner with friends, order take-out, serve it in something stylish and make a ta-da dessert. People eat with their eyes—assemble a mix that channels your personal style and you'll wow them every time.

My entertaining style tends to look formal. I won't go the Victorian route and load up a table with matching china, flatware and glasses on a damask cloth, but I will borrow some of those fancy things—mother-of-pearl forks, monogrammed napkins—to give a table history. Then I mix in secondhand finds and retail steals in unexpected combinations—mid-century goblets with Crate & Barrel stemware; chargers from Christmas Tree Shops with hand-painted dinner plates. The details are dressy, as are some of my guests, but as a host, I set a casual tone, creating tables that are formal but friendly. And when the last Instagram pic is done, we'll put down our phones (and keep them off), raise our glasses up high and party like it's 1900!

Now that you've seen how to mix colors, patterns, periods and materials to infuse your home with personal style, in this chapter you'll use your finds to entertain more inventively than ever before. Consider it the payoff—the party!—the final step on this journey into style that began with the glimmer of discovery and ends with the joy of sharing your creative spirit with others. I organize this chapter into city and country as well—dual points of view from my own journey that I hope can inspire yours. In the city, you'll use your curated basics to create self-serve stations for cocktails and hors d'oeuvres that let you join the party, too. But it's in the country where the real fun begins. Here, you'll take your finds to innovative new heights, mixing multipurpose essentials with decorative details that make an impact on your guests. No matter where you live, or how you entertain, you'll learn how to celebrate your style with confidence.

ENTERTAIN *CITY*

Take some of the work out of playtime with smart shortcuts that make your finds the star.

I can be unpredictable in the city. Sometimes I'll plan a party for days. Other times I'll blurt out to friends, *Hey, come up to the apartment for drinks Wednesday and bring everyone you know!* Then Wednesday hits, and the last thing I want to do is get stuck in the kitchen making fancy hors d'oeuvres from scratch. Personally, I like the styling part—picking out all the pieces for self-serve bars, buffets and cocktail parties with a modern mix. That way, guests help themselves and I can join the party too. Whether you're in the highest high-rise, somewhere in the suburbs or anyplace in between, entertaining in the city is a way of sharing your personal style with people you care about and having fun doing it!

TAKEOUT NIGHT You don't have to cook a thing to host a chic dinner party. Wherever you live, there's bound to be a restaurant, a deli or even just a diner where you can order out. Then use your arsenal of stylish serveware—platters, trays and covered dishes—to create a buffet with a captivating mix. If you're setting a table, do a plated salad or dessert for a more personal touch. LIBATION STATION Drink stations throughout the party scene keep guests circulating. I set up a Prosecco bar by the bookcase (water lily wallpaper by York Wallcoverings) so one of the shelves can hold glassware.

SUSAN SULLY *Houses with Charm*

Dent

APARTMENTS MARIETTE HIMES GOMEZ

PHOTOBIOGRAPHY *Cecil Beaton*

High Style *Legendary Decorators of the Twentieth Century* **Mark Hampton**

JOAN CRAWFORD COWIE

LIVING HOUSES, GARDENS, PEOPLE

20TH-CENTURY DECORATING ARCHITECTURE & GARDENS

BEAUTY AT HOME AERIN LAUDER

AMERICAN DECORATION THOMAS JAYNE

Slim Aarons • A Place in the Sun

POSEIDON ADVENTURE

In culinary school, we made fancy things like *plateaux de fruits de mer.* That's French for "shellfish on a plate" over ice. The dish sits on a stand, adding drama to seafood night. But you needn't serve king crab to wow your guests. Buy frozen shrimp, serve them up high and layer in vegetables. I used vintage silver plate enameled with turquoise and teal, though any modern mix will do. Fabric is Lulu DK; tumblers are CB2.

Put anything on a *PEDESTAL* and it's the fast track to chic.

CRU-TA-DA!

You don't have to buy fruity stars on sticks to make an edible arrangement that gets people talking. This is one of my go-to techniques for dishing up drama with veggies you buy at a grocery store. Behold—the cabbage! It might look the part of Plain Jane next to trendy starlets like kale, but those big, beautiful leaves and waxy, round center can turn simple crudités into a stunning centerpiece. Start with your favorite basket, bowl or compote. Now take a cabbage, peel back the outer leaves to expose the center, cut out a circle from the top and hollow it out with a melon baller. Arrange vegetables in groupings and use the leaves of the cabbage to create layers. Mix up some of your favorite dips, and ta-da! Who's the star now?

DELICIOUS DISH

Nothing beats that Schweddy family recipe, but you can easily find gourmet sausages at grocery stores (chicken! turkey! tofurky!) seasoned any way you like. For a simpler but no less stylish take on the classic charcuterie plate, pick up a few sausages in different flavors and cook them as directed. Next, pull together serving pieces and tableware in a modern mix. You'll need a cutting board or platter, a compote for height, one or two little dishes and a cocktail fork from your arsenal of essentials. Slice the sausages on the diagonal for a fancy look and serve with toasted French bread, grainy mustard and pickles. It's a delicious dish for cocktail parties that's fast, filling and, best of all, self-serve. Just make sure there's enough sausage for the fest.

MAGIC MIRROR

Who's the fairest of them all? You are when you take a chic mirror and use it as a tray. It's glamorous, surprising and a little bit rock star. This mirror is faux bamboo, but find one that reflects your creative spirit. For a quick hors d'oeuvre, I doctored up store-bought biscuit mix with cheddar cheese and chives, then made mini sandwiches with my favorite honey cured ham from Costco.

LET THEM EAT CHEESE

Cheese always brings a smile, and pulling a platter together is easy: Buy one cheddar, the other marbled, cut them into cubes, stick toothpicks into everything (cellophane frill required) and let the good times roll. Not exactly. But it's still easy—if you have a good mix. Start with the cheese. Buy one of each type: soft, firm and blue. Then add a kicker like a flavored goat. Now set the scene and go big! Here, I used a marble tabletop, but any cutting board or tray will work. Add essentials like cake pedestals and compotes to create levels. Layer in flowers or foliage and finish off with a favorite oddball object (here, the obelisk) that gets people talking.

KNIGHT & DAY

It's not often I'll do the sit-down thing in the city. Usually it's some sort of business women's special, where I invite sophisticated, educated, successful career women to talk, um, business. Take this lunch I hosted the first time Jaithan and I met our book editor, Madge. We were already well underway with the project, but I wanted to give her a taste of what was to come. An Indian textile, English lusterware salad plates and fancy monogrammed napkins gave the mix a British Raj vibe. Twin ceramic knights from a chess set kept formalities in check.

ENTERTAIN *COUNTRY*

Throw fancy but friendly parties with a modern mix that celebrates your style.

If entertaining in the city has you pairing take-out menus and self-serve stations to throw spontaneous parties with panache, here is an approach to using your finds that's more considered and creative. In the country, seasons inspire tables that are dressy and detailed, with a blend of elements that bring surprising grandeur to everyday occasions. The china is layered, the glasses are stemmed and the flatware is mixed in modern combinations of vintage and new, rough and refined, simple and elaborate. You can have great fun with your finds in ways that challenge and inspire you to share your style through the seasons.

PERSONAL TOUCH When our friend Colleen came up to the house for a Derby party, she gave us a set of classic mint julep cups personalized just for us from Things Remembered. COCKTAIL ATTIRE Stylish cocktail napkins can make inexpensive wine taste like a fine Bordeaux. Get creative and assemble a set that expresses your bubbly side. Guests crow every time I pull out the roosters; I found five of them at a yard sale. The white set is made from vintage paisley fabric that I had my dry cleaner's seamstress turn into napkins. An English silver-plated toast rack keeps them close at hand.

READY TO ROLL

Bar carts go in and out of fashion, but they'll always have a place in my house. They're two parts chic, one part retro and a splash of camp all rolled into one. I like a bar cart with lots of space and sturdy shelves for piling on a modern mix of glasses, barware and booze. This one is bent bamboo from the '60s that I freshened up with paint. Now it's hot to trot for a Kentucky Derby pre-party in the country with icy mint juleps and Moscow mules.

When the weather warms up, take the *PARTY* outside—furniture and all.

CABANA BOY

I love a casual outdoor party; I'm just not that good at giving one. So when the weather warms up and it's time to celebrate Jaithan's birthday, I take the festivities outside with a dressed-up mix of furniture, tableware and linens. But going formal doesn't have to mean fussy (or expensive!)—if you plan it out. Here's how to throw a fancy dinner party in the great outdoors.

• **SET THE SCENE** Define a space with a rug, a canopy or even a glammed-up umbrella. I used this cabana from Z Gallerie and lined the insides with thrifted twin sheets tied with ribbon. They inspired the palette for the party, from candles down to the foil-wrapped candies.

• **DECORATE IN DETAIL** Dress up the decor by taking indoor furniture outside. I pulled four cushy chairs around a folding table topped with a quilt with an exotic vibe. A bench shakes things up—it says the party doesn't take itself too seriously (and neither should the guests).

• **DISH IT UP** Indoors or out, I always set tables for special occasions—birthdays, holidays, Tuesdays—with a fancy but friendly mix of tableware. Some ironstone plates I scored at an estate sale (page 77) find new digs atop vintage brass chargers. Guests toast the birthday boy in cranberry glass coupes from the '20s; the water tumblers are CB2. Flatware mixes silver and gold, like a David Yurman bracelet.

LYRICAL WRAP

Shards of color on wrapping paper collide with delicate songbirds on Wedgwood china for an outdoor lunch. A trio of Lladró swans I plucked from a thrift shop swim across an abstract sea, their backs billowing with lilacs. I trimmed them of their greens, leaving only the blooms, while in Portuguese bubble vases, I placed single green stems. And when it's done, I'll crumple up the cloth, pair another paper and plate—and do it all again.

JEWEL-EYED DOTTIE

Dottie had a special cake just for birthdays. It was her famous Jell-O Jewel—fruity bits of gelatin suspended in sweet, pineapple-y cream. The colors were always different so each of my brothers and I would feel special. "You're my little gem," she'd say, "and an extra-special gem deserves an extra-special cake." For this little gem, Dottie crammed the cake with as many colors as possible, like a rainbow of balloons in Crayola brights. These days, I'll make Jell-O Jewel cake on my birthday in a sophisticated, tonal palette and serve it with champagne. The plates are chinoiserie and the flatware is brass bamboo. Jaithan bought me the art deco pie server in Paris, its modern brass blade carving a new path through tradition.

I FOUND THESE NAPKINS AT A THRIFT SHOP WHEN I WAS IN HIGH SCHOOL. THE LINEN IS PLAIN; I LOVE HOW THE MONOGRAM POPS.

MIX AND MINGLE

As a kid, I used to think every buffet was the all-you-can-eat kind with endless salad bars and sizzling meats. Then I started working and saw that buffets could be just as chic as any sit-down affair. Buffets are made for mingling, but they don't have to be big to make a statement. Follow these easy tips for setting up simple buffets in style.

• **CREATE A MIX** Start with a show-stopping platter, covered dish or bowl and borrow colors for the rest of the scheme. For this late-summer lap dinner in the country, a fancy English meat dome inspired the trippy tablecloth—contrasting patterns that drive the buffet's aristocrats-on-acid effect. I kept the rest of the pieces neutral, changing up materials, styles and heights.

• **GO WITH THE FLOW** You want to make it easy on your guests, not give them a maze to navigate. Skip the awkward backtracks by planning out a path: plates on one side (here with napkins for grab-and-go ease); high and low sides; entrée with gravy or sauce; and utensils to finish. I always do flatware in celery vases—they show off the handles and add mid-level height. And if you're as neurotic as I am, set out all your serving dishes the night before, labeling each so you don't forget anything.

• **POLISH IT OFF** Don't forget decorator details. Grand elements on a simple buffet are surprising. An antique candlestick updated with colored candles, and garden blooms in a tall vase lend drama. Finishing touches add beauty and utility: a brass crumb tray with brush keeps things tidy.

TURKEY CALL

Dottie had a pair of these pressed glass candy dishes that American company Smith Glass has been making since the '20s. When Thanksgiving came, she'd fill them up with candy corn (and say, "Turkeys like corn") and put them in the living room for little hands like hers to find. When Dottie gave them to me, two became four and four became six, thanks to eBay. Now when I host Thanksgiving, guests always seem to gobble up their soup with a smile.

GLASS WORKS

Flowers don't have to be real to look chic—sometimes a good fake is all you need. Here I used vintage Italian glass flowers in a footed brass compote, then added silver dollar eucalyptus for a natural touch. To make the gilded leaves, I simply spray-painted oak leaves gold and scattered them around the table. Search online marketplaces for other glass centerpieces with a worldly look, like Japanese bonsai.

THANKSGIVING might only be one day, but I think about it all year long. I could be at a flea market or a fabric store in the middle of June and see something fantastic, sparking a flurry of inspiration for a table. This year, after having put up new vintage chintz curtains in the dining room, I saw this gorgeous fabric for a tablecloth at Gray Line Linen in all the same colors. It's almost like natural bark, with a twist. The china picks up the pink-and-teal combo; the smoked-glass goblets and graphite candles carry up the gray. It all added up to an Instagram frenzy to remember—#normanrockwell, #chintz, #modernmix.

HEAVENLY HOLIDAY

When Christmas comes to the farm and snow blankets the pines, I'll open our doors to family and friends for a lavish celebration. In the dining room, floral chintz meets Neapolitan plaid in a pink, white and chocolate brown palette accented with minty greens. For the centerpiece: a French croquembouche summoning guests of every age to sample something sweet.

STACKED COMPOTES,
CAKE PEDESTALS
AND PLATTERS HOLD
HOMEMADE AND STORE-
BOUGHT TREATS ON A
LAYERED LANDSCAPE
WITH MADELEINES,
BROWNIES, PALMIERS,
ITALIAN WEDDING
COOKIES AND CANDIES.

EGG-CELLENT EGGNOG

Now is no time to count calories; when it comes to eggnog, the richer the better. I start with a good store-bought, like Jack Daniels, add two pints of Häagen-Dazs vanilla bean ice cream, pile on homemade whipped cream, then top it off with toasted coconut, cinnamon and nutmeg— all in a footed brass punch bowl with a modern mix of coupes, cups and glasses. As far as booze goes, I keep it on the side and let the big kids play mixologist.

DOCTOR IT UP

Pair store-bought confections and gourmet ingredients to make simple desserts that stand out from the crowd. For instance, sandwich gourmet raspberry jam between madeleines for a festive fruity combination. Top brownie bites with chocolate-covered espresso beans and dust with confectionary sugar. Got a go-to restaurant with a dessert that's to die for? I asked my favorite to bottle up their caramel sauce for spooning over rosettes. Store-bought cheesecake goes to the ball dressed in toasted coconut coating, and the store-bought pound cake I turned into petit fours and covered with a coral-y fondant glaze.

LAYER ON STYLE

Create a gorgeous dessert table by layering curated essentials, like platters, cake pedestals and compotes in stacked combinations. And pay attention to proportion—compotes shouldn't overwhelm cake pedestals beneath. Pile treats in neat stacks and casual mounds. If you entertain for a crowd, turn your dining table into a right-height buffet by putting it on bed risers. Buy or have made a floor-length cloth in a neutral linen, then swap out table toppers from season to season.